FREE OR CHEAP
ACTIVITIES, DINING, & TRAVEL

WILLIAM & STEPHANIE LASKA

i

KAUAI CHEAP VACATIONS

Authors:

Bill "Willy Willy" & Stephanie "Kekepania" Laska

Contributing Keiki Authors: Charlotte & Alexander Laska

Photography by Stephanie Laska

Printed with sorrow from the Mainland,

with dreams of permanent relocation to Kaua'i

ISBN: 9781549832284

Imprint: Independently published

Dedication

In 2002, my sweetheart and I floated around a romantic four-acre pool under the moonlight. We had traveled to Kaua'i for free of course, and were paying half the rate of other hotel guests.

It was the eve of my 30th birthday, and even though the trip was technically my present, Bill pulled me into his arms and whispered oh so eloquently,

"Do you want to get a rock or what?"

The next day we purchased my engagement band, tiny diamonds in the shape of five hibiscus flowers at the resort jewelry store, and our obsession with Kaua'i began.

Kaua'i Cheap Vacations is dedicated to all the cheapskates out there with a dream of visiting paradise, AKA "Ballers on a Budget."

Preface

Do you dream of visiting the beautiful island of Kaua'i, but fear the experience will rob your piggy bank? Do you not have the time to research articles and reviews about where to stay and what to do on your trip?

It is possible to have the trip of a lifetime on a limited budget.

Our family has done the research for you! We have vacationed to Kaua'i for over 20 years, in many capacities, *all on the cheap*!

We have traveled as:

*Single folks without kids! "Whoop-whoop"
*For our engagement - Romance!
*Family with small babies - Newborn and a 2-year-old!
(yes, we were THOSE people on the plane)
*Family with our tweens children (ages 12 and 10)
*With our senior-age parents (they won't let us say how old)
*With groups of teenagers (and survived!)
*In a family reunion (with just under a dozen folks)

Kaua'i Cheap Vacations provides up-to-date information on how to save money on your trip. We have researched every aspect of your vacation and are willing to share secret tips on how to save money, all while having the trip of a lifetime!

We will share with you tips and suggestions on how to enjoy your days in paradise for free or very little money.

Maybe you want to save a chunk of change to splurge on a helicopter ride or a five-star dinner once during your trip? Or maybe you blew your budget just getting to Kaua'i and have little leftover? Either way, we promise you will enjoy the island without maxing out your credit card.

*Enjoy free Polynesian dancing performances
*Listen to local musicians for free or at very low cost
*Bring home souvenirs for a fraction of the listed price
*Save huge amounts of money for big ticket activities
*Experience the same resorts and beaches as enjoyed by movie stars
*Dine in the fanciest restaurants for a portion of the cost as other diners
*Explore the island like a local
*Discover unusual and unique activities not advertised for tourist

How does that sound? Let's get started!

Charity

Proceeds from this book, Kauai Cheap Vacations, benefit our favorite charity in Hawaii, the Kauai Humane Society.

Be sure to check out Chapter 8 "Great for Kids" where we explain how to take a Kauai dog on a field trip during your vacation. Even if you don't have kids with you, I promise this will be the highlight of your vacation – and its FREE!

Disclaimer

No part of this eBook may be reproduced or transmitted in any form or by any means, electronic or mechanical, including photocopying, recording or by any information storage and retrieval system, without written permission from the author.

The information provided within this eBook is for general informational purposes only. While we try to keep the information up-to-date and correct, there are no representations or warranties, express or implied, about the completeness, accuracy, reliability, suitability or availability with respect to the information, products, services, or related graphics contained in this eBook for any purpose. Any use of this information is at your own risk.

We recognize that there are more free or cheap activities in Kaua'i than are included in this book. This may be due to the fact that our family didn't like the activity or location or have yet to try it out. If you would like your business or idea to be considered for next year's edition, we welcome your direct feedback. Please contact the authors at: KauaiCheapVacations@gmail.com.

The information contained within this eBook is strictly for entertainment purposes. If you wish to apply ideas or activities contained in this eBook, you are taking full responsibility for your actions.

The author has made every effort to ensure the accuracy of the information within this book was correct at time of publication. The author does not assume and hereby disclaims any liability to any party for any loss, damage, or disruption caused by errors or omissions, whether such errors or omissions result from accident, negligence, or any other cause.

Table of Contents

CHAPTER   1
Transportation

Airline Travel

The biggest expense of your trip to Hawaii is airfare. Or is it? Here are some tips and tricks to get the cost of air travel to Lihue Airport in Kaua'i (LIH) significantly reduced or eliminated.

Hawaiian Airlines Credit Card

Who wants a free airline ticket to Hawaii? And what about half off for a companion? At the time of publication, the Hawaiian Airlines Credit Card from Chase offers a huge signing bonus of 30,000 miles (40,000+ needed for a flight from the mainland, and much less for inter-island flights). Additionally, card holders receive a free checked bag when flying Hawaiian when the ticket is purchased using the card. That's a $25 savings right there! The biggest reason for becoming a card holder (aside from how pretty it looks in your wallet) is the "half off companion flight" you receive once a year. This benefit offsets the annual fee charged by Chase. You also get one mile for every dollar charged on the card so we recommend charging all your expenses on the card that you may have previously paid with a debit card or personal check. It goes without saying that you have to pay the balance in full every month to avoid the interest fees that will be charged. Pay special attention to utility bills and the like that charge a fee when paid with a credit card. Interest charges and credit card fees will erode any benefit that the free miles give you so stay sharp and don't be taken by the credit card company!!

After you enjoy your vacation to Kaua'i, be sure to pay off any remaining balance on your card and CANCEL it! Next year, your spouse or travel partner can sign up for the card and reap the rewards. We call this the "credit card shuffle". Chase allows you to sign up for the card again to earn their current bonus (30,000 miles) 24 months AFTER cancellation, so be sure to note the date you cancelled in your calendar alerts on your phone to sign up again. Yes, it's a bit of a hassle, but the benefits are clear: save hundreds of dollars and be able to return to Kaua'i year after year!

Alaska Airlines Credit Card (Virgin Airlines now owned by Alaska Airlines)

In addition to the large deposit of loyalty points upon making the required charges in the first 3 months, a free companion ticket is issued the first year with a regularly priced flight purchase. You also get a free checked bag when flying Alaska Airlines (when ticket is purchased with your card). The Visa Signature Credit Card from Bank of America offers a companion fare for $99 (mainland to Hawaii included) with a regular priced purchase. This benefit offsets the annual fee charged by the bank.

Of course, the credit card programs change regularly, so this would be an example of their current offering. You will need to check their website for up to the minute promotions.

Airline Reservations (paying cash, not with points)

If you are frustrated by the cash price of airlines tickets from your hometown direct to Kaua'i, try thinking about a different airport, like Honolulu! Yes, this is a different island (Oahu) altogether, but more flights will be available at a lower price. You can always book a separate inter-island flight from Oahu (HNL) to Lihue, Kaua'i (LIH) for a fraction of the cost(usually under $100 one way) . Be sure to allow enough time to change terminals if needed and even a trip out/back through security if you need to pick up luggage. Yes, this is an absolute hassle. If it makes the difference of hundreds if not thousands of dollars for your airline tickets, isn't it worth it?

When looking at booking your flights, here are a few more tips. Weekday flights are usually cheaper than weekend fares. Selecting "flexible dates" or "include nearby airports" may also provide discounts for your flights. Next, click on "calendar view" on the airline's website to examine which days offer the cheapest flights. Lastly, if you are flexible, avoid traveling to Kaua'i during "high season" whenever schools are on holiday (Christmas break, Spring break, Summer break, etc.) as the prices are much higher!

Luggage

With most airlines charging $25 - $50 per bag for check-in luggage, this topic is worth considering. These little charges add up, especially when traveling in a group. Let's take a look at how to eliminate, reduce, and maximize checked baggage fees.

Free baggage check

No matter what your airline preference, be sure to check the company website to determine what loopholes allow you to check a bag for free. Do you need to be a mileage club or other loyalty club member? Sign up for a no-annual fee credit card? (Note I said no annual fee!) We make sure at least one person in our party will receive a free checked bag. Of course, we check in our largest suitcase and carefully weigh it at home to prevent overweight charges (more than 50lbs). We each bring a carry-on suitcase and backpack on the plane to further stretch our budget. The backpacks come in handy for hikes and car trips, where everyone is responsible for packing their own drinks, snacks, and activities.

Active military (especially in uniform) will likely enjoy free checked luggage no matter what the airline.

Food in your Suitcase?

You might laugh at this one, but with the price of food so high in Kaua'i, why not offset the expense by packing food in your suitcase to enjoy. We fill an entire suitcase (carry on the airplane, so not to incur charges) with dry goods to enjoy during the trip. Dried fruit, nuts, granola bars, tortillas, peanut butter, cereal, dried pasta, and rice will cost so much less from your grocery store back home than in Hawaii. TSA might have a good laugh when inspecting my luggage but my embarrassment is short lived when I feed my family on the cheap.

If you are staying in a condo during your vacation, be sure to research what will be provided in your unit. Usually a starter kit of dish soap, bar soap, and laundry soap is provided, but beyond the first washing, you are expected to provide your own. Sometimes the previous renters leave behind a stash of these frequently used items, but it's not something you can count on. These are easy and inexpensive items to pack in your suitcase that will save you hassle and expense:

Ziploc bags
Garbage bags
Laundry soap packets
Shampoo and conditioner
Bar Soap

Parking

Getting to and from the airport can add significant charges to your vacation.

Park N Fly

An unexpected and unfair part of traveling to the islands is paying for your car to be babysat upon your return. We have uncovered a few ways to "cheat the system" and save on the backend. Many large hotel chains offer a "stay, park and fly" package if you spend just one night at their hotel! LaQuinta, Marriott, Hilton, Holiday Inn and Ramada are just a few to explore. In addition to reducing the stress of traveling to the airport the day of your flight, you will enjoy a convenient free shuttle ride from the hotel to your gate after a free breakfast. Now that's traveling in style!

Public Transit

If you live near a public transit system, you might also be able to book a long-term parking spot at a station far away from the airport. The parking spots at our rapid transit system are booked online months in advance, and are a fraction of the cost of airport parking rates. The only hiccup we have experienced is that our public transit doesn't run 24/7; verify your flight times coincide with public transit so you aren't calling for a taxi!

Don't be surprised to see lawn chairs next to bus stops. This unique tradition continues all over the island!

Ride Share

Lastly, you might have a friend or family member that lives closer to your departing airport and wouldn't mind having your car parked out front of their house. Lyft or Uber can give you online estimates of service from their house to the airport, and saves the awkward conversation of begging your friend to drive you to the airport. No one likes to be asked that favor!

Upon Arrival in Kaua'i

Lei Greeting

You might be inclined to add on a lei greeting to your package when arriving on the island. We beg you to save that $30 charge (per lei!) and make a trip to your local dollar store. Buy colorful silk leis for your entire family and enjoy wearing them throughout your vacation for just a dollar each! See the "lei making" section later in this book.

Some of the fancier resorts on the island actually provide a complimentary fresh flower lei upon arrival for their guests. We like to enjoy this perk while "visiting" the Grand Hyatt in Poipu. Mahalo!

Rental Car Savings

The rental car is usually the third largest expense, just under hotel and flight. We have found that COSTCO offers competitive pricing, without a charge for additional drivers. Tip: Once you have made your car reservation, check back frequently as the price often changes! Costco members do not physically pay for the car rental until at the car rental counter in Kaua'i, so beforehand, you are able to grab a better price if you see it advertised without a penalty of cancelation/change. Last year we were able to save $150 simply by checking the website again prior to our trip!

Loyalty programs or memberships

Be sure to utilize other discounts based on loyalty programs or membership groups. For example: USAA, AAA, Military, Airlines loyalty programs, etc. all have unique "promo codes" that provide additional savings at check out. You can even google the name of your car rental agency and "promo code" to uncover a variety of promotions. After some trial and error of copying and pasting codes, you will definitely realize a savings!

Additionally, we recommend reserving the smallest car available. These are usually the most popular with tourists, and therefore the car rental agencies "run out of cars" in that category upon your arrival, resulting in a complimentary upgrade! Even if that is not the case, you are able to negotiate the price for upgrades at the rental car counter. Tip: Steer clear of convertibles and open-air Jeeps – it's going to be hot, sunny, and rainy during your stay, and you will need shade and air conditioning! Check your car insurance policy prior to your trip to review rental car coverage. You will save mucho-dinero bypassing all of the additional coverage presented to you at time of rental.

Lastly, be sure to say, "YES, THANK YOU," when the car attendant asks if you would like a free map. Most of us are so used to our smart phones for help with directions that the thought of a paper map might seem archaic! Be forewarned that cell coverage can be spotty in parts of the island (Waimea canyon, Hanalei), so having an old-school paper map might come in handy. You don't want to get lost and have to find a public payphone – yes, they still have those in Kaua'i!

Uber and Lyft

Sorry, urbanites, but last time we checked there were SO FEW Uber driver on the island of Kaua'i! Maybe that can be your side job on the island? That being said, you might not want to rely on Uber or Lyft for your sole source of transportation. Aloha Wiki Shuttle

808.651.9945 Doug

The Aloha Spirit Shuttle is a decorated open-air vehicle available in the Poipu area for free! (Caveat - We recommend a hefty tip to help keep Doug in business.) Similar to a taxi service, contact the Aloha Spirit Shuttle to arrange transportation in and around the Poipu area. You might feel like a guest on Gilligan's Island when the wiki shuttle pulls up! There are no seat belts or doors, so hold onto your little ones or inebriated friends. The shuttle has the feel of a large-scale golf cart. What a great way to enjoy a few Mai Tais during dinner without the worry of stumbling home in the dark.

CHAPTER 2:
Accommodations

Hotel

U ndeniably, your two largest expenditures on your Hawaiian trip will be airfare and accommodations. Over the years, we have used a number of tactics to avoid paying the exorbitant rates that most of hotels charge on the island. Here is a list of our findings:

Consider a non-oceanfront hotel that is still nice, safe and convenient to popular destinations. We use the typical hotel price shopping sites on the internet (KAYAK, Priceline, Expedia, Bookings, Trivago, etc.). You can always walk to the beach or jump in the car for a short drive.

Next, we have found that quite often there are popular hotels being renovated and updated but are still open for business. The unaffected rooms in the property can be booked at a reduced cost since the management knows that there will be noise or dust issues, or perhaps just a closed amenity like a spa or pool (big resorts have several). Most of the time these discounted rooms pop up on your internet search at such a low cost that it will give you a hint that something is up.

By far our most used ploy to save money is the hotel reward points system employed to maintain loyalty. Choose a company that you wish to use (Hyatt/Marriott) and use them consistently for your other stays and business trips, if you travel for work, to rack up loyalty points. Most importantly, open one of their loyalty credit cards and earn an immediate lump sum deposit of reward points. To get the large deposit of points upfront, most cards will want you to spend between $1000 to $4000 in the first few months. (This same strategy applies to the major airlines and we usually like to open one of these cards

every so often and pay all of our bills through it in order to hit the minimum). Some of them are hard to reach for us like the $4000 in 4 months because, as you can probably tell, we are CHEAP and enjoy BARGAINS! But when planned properly, it can be done. We have timed the paying of our kids braces in the past to meet these minimums and of course, the unexpected medical bill or the unplanned kitchen appliance that goes bonkers on you will help also. It goes without saying that these minimums must be paid off in a timely manner or else any gain from the points earned will be erased by the accruing interest charges.

A specific example of a current benefit is with the Hyatt Chase Visa. After "spending" the required minimum during the introductory period, a voucher is issued to the cardholder for two complimentary nights at any Hyatt. You could then utilize your two nights free at the Grand Hyatt Kaua'i, arguably one of the nicest Hyatt properties in their entire worldwide fleet of hotels. FOR FREE!

In our travels, every so often we visit a hotel and we are not satisfied with the service. If this is an obvious case of the hotel providing bad service or a bad product (plumbing issues, construction noise, closed pools, elevator repairs) then do not hesitate to call the front desk as soon as possible to let them know and in a lot of cases, you will get a reduction in your room charge or money off on a future visit. Do not let them talk you into moving into another room to solve the problem; this simple task can take hours and who wants to bother with that when you're on vacation? Plus, now you have wasted half a day and you may not get your reduction in rate or free room on a future visit.

Discount programs

If you are booking your hotel directly, be sure to ask for all discounts that may apply. Do you work for the government? Active or retired military? AAA? AARP? Or maybe the company you work for has a negotiated rate with this chain. Hotel rates are all negotiable, so pick up the phone and ask for a discount.

Condo

Our favorite! Condo living is an excellent way to save on accommodations on your Hawaii trip. Condos for rent can be found by doing a quick internet search. There are only a handful of large property managers on Kaua'i that broker "vacation rental condos". While ocean front condos may be close in price to an oceanfront hotel room in a 4-5-star hotel, there are additional benefits to consider. Remember that the condo will have a kitchen; if you are staying over 5 or 6 days (my limit for consecutive meals eaten at a restaurant), then a kitchen will save you A LOT of money and will also help with your waistline since who doesn't eat a little extra or a little more recklessly when at a restaurant on vacation. Close parking is also a big benefit. The self-parking at the large hotel resorts is very far away and who wants to lug groceries through the main lobby of a hotel and down the myriad hallways? Additionally, having a little more space to "stretch out" will help your family or group to unwind and have privacy without being constantly on top of each other.

Even if you don't plan on "cooking" in your condo, you will enjoy the refrigerator to hold drinks, snacks, and "leftovers." Since bugs are plentiful on the island, the refrigerator is a safe place to maintain freshness and warehouse cereal, crackers, and any boxed snacks you may have packed in your suitcase.

Property managers specializing in "vacation rentals"

Kaua'i Vacation Rentals, www.Kauaivacationrentals.com (808) 245-8841 is one of the biggest brokers of condo rentals for Kaua'i. The knowledgeable staff can assist you with small or large groups within a wide variety of budgets.

Room Finding Services

AIR BNB

Rent entire homes or just a room throughout Kauai.

VRBO

Book a vacation rental unit directly from the owner.

CHAPTER 3: Hiking

The reason you bought this book was to uncover free or very cheap activities for your vacation. Unless specified otherwise, the majority of shared activities are at no charge to you! Please consider when reading our shared suggestions that this is by no means an exhausted list of every single free thing to do on the island. We are simply sharing our favorites based on our own experiences at the time of publication.

The beauty of Kaua'i is all around you. I beg you to leave your resort or condo and set foot on a dirt path and explore the native island. The experience of walking through a genuine jungle and looking up to see a canopy of lush greenery is unlike any experience you've ever had. Of course, mountains, canyons, waterfalls and the ocean are pretty too.

There are various levels of hikes available for all ages and abilities, so do not be intimidated! You can always turn around, slow down, or break your group up into different paces/skill levels.

Kalalau Trail

Highway 560, North Shore

Let's start with the Kalalau Trail as it is the pinnacle of all free activities in Kaua'i. Even if you only experience the drive to the Kalalau Trail and only walk for 0.25 miles to the first look out, you won't be disappointed. It's the most magical and beautiful destination on the island.

Ke'e Beach serves as the starting point for the Kalalau Trail. The road you travel to Ke'e Beach is like a scene from Jurassic Park. Everything is so beautiful and lush; be prepared to drive over narrow roads and even one-way, one-lane bridges. Cell service is spotty along this route, so have an old-fashioned paper map available to help you navigate. Maps are plentiful and free in travel brochures in every hotel/restaurant lobby. Also, your rental car agency can provide a map at no charge.

Ke'e Beach and the Kalalau Trail begins at the very end of the road. The infamous Napali Coastline takes over where the road ends and is only accessible on foot, overhead in a helicopter/plane, or on boat. We of course, choose the least expensive route, on foot!

The Napali Coastline is a 15 mile stretch of pristine beauty where the mountain range ends abruptly at the shoreline in a display of dramatic cliffs. Untouched by civilization, the dramatic sheer cliffs are not like anything you have ever seen. Waterfalls and emerald green pinnacles wrap the entire northwest stretch of remote Hawaii. This is a must see for all visitors!

On our first visit to the Kalalau Trail, we arrived about 920ish, which is pretty late by hiking standards. For late arrivals, parking is awful. There is an ample sized dirt parking lot near Ke'e Beach; however, it fills up fast. To add to your adventure, the parking area is quite rocky and full of large swells. Jeeps or trucks won't feel a thing but sedans are in for quite a shock. Some fearful visitors simply parallel park along the street. Lesson learned, arrive earlier to secure a parking spot and have the benefits of cooler weather and less people to contend with.

A clean public restroom and outdoor shower area is adjacent to the parking lot. Fill your water bottles and bring more than you anticipate needing. There is no support once you are out on the trail other than passing hikers. Signage recommends a minimum of 2 liters of water per person.

The Kalalau Trailhead is across the street from the restrooms. It is a well-marked trailhead with distances posted for each landmark of the trail (see photos). Distances are one way. Plan on 1-2 hours per 2 miles of hiking, depending on weather and your abilities. While this may seem obvious, you don't have to hike the entire trail. We have "hiked" the Kalalau Trail twice now and have not passed the 2mile mark! The breathtaking views at the beginning of the hike make a hike of any distance worth it. You have to be flexible and realistic when hiking with 2 kids under the of 13. Enjoy the experience for as long as you feel comfortable, then turn around to make it back for aloha hour.

Ke'e Beach View, .25 miles

Coast Viewpoint, .5 miles

Hanakapi'ai, 2 miles

Hanakapi'ai Falls, 4 miles

Hanakoa, 6 miles

Kalalau, 11 miles

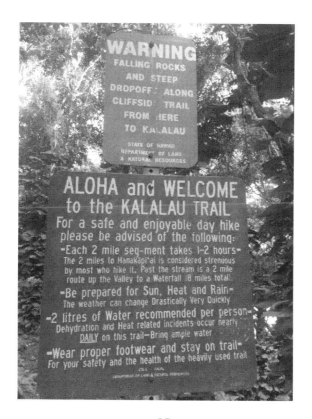

Hoopii Falls Hike

5800 Kapahi Rd., Kapaa

Super easy and enjoyable hike as long as you douse yourself in bug spray before and during your hike! This is a nice little hike although it has a tricky entrance through a barbed wire fence and no signage.

Once you get on the dirt trail, you're transported into what looks like a jungle movie set. The trail is mostly clear but there are trees, vines, plants, ferns and more flora all around you --BUGS TOO.

Take a right at the creek and follow it downhill. You will not miss the waterfalls. Be careful in the wet clay going down the hill it gets super slick! You will arrive at the first waterfall in about a 10-minute walk. This is the waterfall where many people have jumped off from the top. Make sure there is someone experienced with you to tell you where the right jump-off spot is, or better yet, stay safely on land! There may be rocks down there. Keep hiking further, about 10 - 15 minutes longer, and you access another larger waterfall, complete with a rope swing (if you can figure out how to access that side of the river). To find the rope swing and swimming area, hike about 30 meters or so past the second falls.

To the second waterfall and back is about 2 miles, mostly flat and shaded.

Nice area and not very busy.

View of the trailhead.

The Wai Koa Loop Trail

Anaina Hou Community Park

5-2723 Kuhio Highway, Kilauea, HI

Good clean fun in Kaua'i. Located on the north side by Hanalei, my family and I very much enjoyed this 5-mile loop hike. A must see is the dam and waterfall at about mile two. We took some of our best selfies of our whole trip to the island here with the man-made waterfall in the background. Walk around the perimeter of the waterfall and you will find a natural bamboo forest, Buddha tribute, and even a rope swing. This beautiful hike is well marked, flat and free!

We walked the Anaina Hou Trail, but you can alternately explore the path on mountain bikes (rents for about $25 a pop for six hours). At the bike rental counter, you will also find a beautiful & clean miniature golf course and a great coffee bar on site that includes ice cream, shave ice and snack foods. In addition to the unbelievably beautiful dam near the middle of the hike, we also saw horses close up and personal. Located right off the main road to Hanalei.

Entering the parking lot, you will encounter this fun "ALOHA" display made out of flowers. The small store offers maps of the hike. The trailhead starts back behind the recycling center.

Clean single bathrooms available and a hose to wash the mud off your shoes.

Makawehi Lithified Cliffs

Just past the Grand Hyatt Hotel Ainako Road, Poipu

Inside the shady trees dotting the shores of Shipwreck Beach lies an easy-to-follow curvy path. Follow the trail heading North East (toward Lihue) and soon you will begin a gentle climb up the cliff. My young children and senior-aged parents completed this without much strain or complaining (even in flip flops!) so don't let this short hike scare you. That being said, make sure not to leave your shoes behind as the path along the crest of the cliff can be rocky. At the top of the path you will be rewarded with panoramic views of the Keoneloa Bay that are jaw-dropping. The rock formations jut out over the

The Makauwahi Cave Reserve (Sinkhole) is about 2 miles from the beginning of the trail. Following the signs, it is located no more than 100 feet or so inland. The cave is open for tours on Monday, Wednesday and Fridays. A docent can show you around for a suggested $10 per person donation. We explored the Makauwahi Cave Reserve when it is technically "closed" (i.e. free!) and you can pretty much enjoy everything this destination has to offer.

If you're driving, continue on the dirt road past the Grand Hyatt, which goes onto the Grove Farm property (access is permitted - just don't park or wander on their private property). The dirt road is easily accessible via a four-wheel drive vehicle with plenty of clearance, but the pitted craters in the road towards the end are so big even the jeeps were having trouble navigating through. Instead, turn right on the road that leads to the horse-riding stables, bear to the left and park along the fence. There will be other cars there already. From that spot walk towards the water a little way, then turn left and you'll find the marked path toward the cave.

ocean like an Olympic high dive. The wind howls and you will feel like an ancient Hawaiian King.

Follow the trail along the cliffs and you will experience breathtaking sights and a sink hole, hidden beaches, and of course, cliffs! The flat trail is a couple miles long and hugs the coastline. Return the way you came in or explore inland trails.

Land Tortoises are located outside the cave entrance across a small bridge. There is a flat area that looks like a farm and is set up with large fenced-in areas for the animals. The tortoises are slowly walking around their arenas munching on wild plants.

Kalapaki Circle\Mansions on Nawiliwili Bay

Kalapaki Beach, Lihue

This short hike has become a staple of ours every time we come to hang out on Kalapaki Beach. Perhaps we should call this a stroll, and not a hike, as you are walking on pavement?

Public access to Kalapaki Beach is providing with a public access parking lot on the site of the Kaua'i Marriott. Once you arrive on the beach, head eastward toward the cliffs (toward the airport) you will come to a public restroom and an elevator which will take you up one level to Kalapaki Circle. Not sure why this elevator is even here because it seems that few people know about it, and even fewer use it. If you hang a right, you can walk down the dead-end road past all the beautiful mansions that overhang the cliff over Nawiliwili Bay.

Over the years, we have seen many of these homes remodeled or even combined into mega mansions. Wouldn't it be fun to buy one of these after winning the lottery? At the end of Kalapaki Circle is an area where the public can park with very few spots. This is a beautiful area to explore with vista views of the bay, lighthouse, and coastline. Continue your walk through the Kaua'i Lagoons along the coastline, described next.

Very accessible hike/walk for all abilities and ages.

Kaua'i Lagoons

*3610 Rice St, Lihue*Off the public parking lot for the Kaua'i Beach Marriott is the beginning of another "unofficial" short hike to the Kaua'i Lagoons and the beautiful cliffs and beaches (beyond that border, the airport). The beginning of this hike is through the Kaua'i Beach Marriott golf course so you must stay on the assigned golf cart path. This cart path is the state mandated public beach access path, so do not feel intimidated by

the golfers. On the other hand, do not leave the path and walk on the golf course. There have been some failed businesses on the grounds around the lagoons (including a nightclub where we celebrated our engagement!) with the current project looking like a large hotel with residences on site.

Sleeping Giant Hike

East Trail Haleilio Rd, Kapaa

West Trail Nounou Rd

The Sleeping Giant Trail is named such because of the profile seen along the ridges of the mountain top – at just the right angle the trees and rocks form the face of a giant laying on his back, facing the sky.

The Sleeping Giant Trail above Kapa'a town is a relatively moderate climb, with plenty of views at and near the top. Bring water, because it's warm and humid, and be ready for muddy and slippery parts towards the bottom. I must admit it was a bit steeper than we expected. We hiked to the top and took in the sweeping views of Kaua'i from the head of the giant. It was about a two hour hike up and back - well worth the effort! Hikers should wear hiking shoes or at least tennis shoes - even when dry, debris on the trail can make it slippery and easy to lose your footing. Some scrambling with your hands to make it up part of the mountain, but nothing too extreme. My young children actually got a

real kick out of that part as they became mini-rock climbers around a bend or two. There are actually 3 different paths leading up to the top, where there are benches at lookout points and some picnic tables for hikers to rest and eat at the top.

There is no public restroom or water so plan ahead. We were also surprised to find the climate changed during our hike, with a surprise rain shower that added to the excitement and fun.

There are so many hikes to enjoy in Kauai, we aren't able to list them all! We share only our favorites and those that are safe. Some of our hikes have been complete failures (getting lost, sliding down mountains, covered in bug bites, etc.) and we do not want to promote anything you won't enjoy. An example of such a hike was this recent attempt at hiking to the bottom of the Wailua Falls (not an authorized path). The hike was so slippery that my entire family refused to hike any more for the rest of the vacation.

CHAPTER 4:
Swinging Bridges

Swinging Bridge of Hanapepe

3857 Hanapepe Rd, Hanapepe

ho doesn't want to experience walking across a suspended wooden bridge in the middle of the jungle? This free and exhilarating experience is a must for anyone with a little boy (or who is a little boy at heart). With every step, the bridge creaks, shifts, and sways. It's like being transported into the heart of an Indiana Jones movie!

There are a few swinging bridges on the island. First, the well-known swinging bridge of Hanapepe, easily accessible next to the Aloha Spice Company. It was built first in the 1900s, but later damaged and restored after Hurricane Iniki in 1992. This is the most popular and well kept swinging bridge on Kaua'i and is easily accessible within a short walk of the parking lot in Hanapepe.

Waimea Swinging Bridge of West Kaua'i

Second, there is a lesser known and harder to find swinging bridge: the Waimea Swinging Bridge of West Kaua'i. Head west on Highway 50 from Hanapepe and take a right onto Menehune Road (before mile marker 23). After a short drive through a neighborhood, you will discover the Waimea Swinging Bridge on your right. This bridge is not well published or talked about. On our drive to explore the Waimea Swinging Bridge we even encountered wild horses milling about the narrow road!

Lastly, the Koinobori Display and Kapaia Swinging Bridge must be mentioned as we wrap up this section, but only in haste. Though advertised, the Kapaia Bridge is blocked off and not open to the public. You can see it, but not walk across it. There is a beautiful display of windsocks, however, called the "Koinobori Display," and can be viewed at *4453 Laukini Rd., Lihue*.

Rope Swings

Let me start by saying I do not recommend jumping or swinging into shallow water! This is a risky activity, and while you might feel like Tarzan, I urge you to be safe and cautious. The following rope swing locations are not sponsored by a business or organization. They have not been vetted for safety. Swing at your own risk. In addition to rocks/debris, consider flesh-eating bacteria may be present in fresh water. Really!

Wailua River (past Fern Grotto, Secret Falls Hike)

Kipu Falls, eastern Kaua'i

Kilauea Stream where it empties into bay at Kahili beach

Wai Koa Loop Trail – Stone Dam (trail starts at miniature golf) and is pictured here in book

Tire Swing – along paved bike path

During your hikes, you will also come across strong vines hanging in the jungle. Really! Test these out and take one for a swing.

CHAPTER 5: Driving & Lazy Days

he beautiful lush greenery of Kaua'i is fed from frequent, tropical rainstorms. The best part is that storms don't usually last long, and you might find the rain refreshing on a hot day. On the flip side, when you are stuck in a rainstorm, another part of the island is experiencing full sun. We usually plan our adventures based on the weather, reserving the full sun days for the beach by our residence, and rainy days to jump in the car and explore another "sunnier" part of Kaua'i. (Tip: add multiple cities to your weather app to monitor weather on the north, south, and eastern parts of Kaua'i).

Polihale State Park

Hwy 50, Waimea

If you choose just one adventure during your vacation, enjoy the sunset from Polihale beach. The unkempt road to Polihale might make your regret this decision, but if your rental car survives the adventure, you will not regret seeing the most amazing beach in Hawai'i. The magnitude of the sand, the waves and the cliffs are simply magical; bucket list moment!

We have ventured down the "road to Polihale" many times and have survived, all while driving a regular sedan without four-wheel drive. I will note, however, that we drove this route during hot and dry weather. If it was wet or muddy, I would have turned around, or risked being stuck in the middle of nowhere!

Once you arrive at the "Polihale State Park" sign you are faced with two choices. We recommend veering toward the right on the final stretch of road to parallel the beach. There are multiple turn offs along this road entering the dunes which offer campsites, a simple public bathroom and an outdoor shower area. Be aware of where you park your car to prevent getting stuck in the loose sand.

You can also choose to drive to the literal "end of the road" where majestic Napali cliffs terminate this mile long, pristine beach. Pack an umbrella and a towel to sit on, and plan to spend some time. If you are quiet enough, you might even hear the guttural "baaing" noise of the goats that live on the cliffs to your right.

This is not a swimming beach. Beware of the waves! I was frolicking with my son in the waist high surf when a monster wave came out of nowhere and knocked us down. There is a strong undertow and unexpected wave pattern at Polihale Beach. Swimming is not recommended! If you wear glasses, heed my advice and purchase a set of Croakies or similar sunglass strap that will prevent your glasses from washing off your head into oblivion. (True story: my twin brother lost his glasses from an unexpected wave and had to wear my prescription sunglasses – during the day and night -- just so he could see!)

Drive by Waterfalls

Only in Kaua'i can you literally drive up, park, and see a waterfall without even getting out of your car! There are waterfalls everywhere in Kaua'i, but these are the two easy "must dos".

Wailua Falls

Ma'alo Rd Hwy 583. Lihue, HI

Opaeka'a Falls

Kuamoo Road (580) from highway 56

If these "drive by" waterfalls wet your whistle, then maybe you are up for a bigger challenge? The Kalalau Trail offers "walk through" waterfalls and even an amazing 300-foot waterfall via a strenuous hike to Hanakapaiai Falls.

Russian Fort Elizabeth State Historical Park

Highway 50, Waimea, Kaua'i, HI 96766

The well-marked turn-off is labeled a historical fort, but you might be surprised not to find a structure. Only part of the fort was even finished (1815-1817) when the Russians were ordered to leave the island and the buildings were destroyed. History aficionados (like us) might find this site of Hawaiian history interesting, so if history isn't your cup of tea, drive on.

On the opposite side of the ruins (ocean side) there is a really nice view over Waimea Bay. This is worth a stop, especially before sunset. Some say the beach here is close to a "black sand beach" due to volcanic rock influence. The purple or dark sand is unusual, and though rugged, we really enjoyed exploring this location. Be prepared that this landmark appears to be an area where the local fishermen hang out, and sadly, quite a bit of trash and litter is strewn about.

Ninini Point Lighthouse

Ninini Point St., Lihue, Kaua'i, HI

The Ninini Point Lighthouse is well worth the visit if you are a fan of lighthouses! Note: this is not the Kilauea lighthouse in North shore seen on most travel brochures of Kaua'i.

This little-known gem is in Lihue. It's not easy to find as there are no obvious road signs. Use your phone/GPS to plug in Ninini Point Lighthouse, and the directions will take you to a drivable dirt road. Be aware though, that this is a one car in-and-out kind of dirt road, so if another car is going the opposite direction, one will have to back out for the other to go thru. There are drive offs, but these may be challenging for the inexperienced. Otherwise, the dirt road is walkable, less than a mile. The lighthouse is very close to the airport, right under the flight path of landing and departing planes! Whether on foot or in your vehicle, once you arrive at the Ninini Point Lighthouse, you will be rewarded with beautiful ocean vistas and the confidence that very few others have enjoyed this unique, free experience.

Kaua'i Coffee Plantation

870 Halewili Rd., Kalaheo

Who doesn't like free coffee? The Kaua'i Coffee Plantation is a must do for all caffeine lovers. The best part? Free tour and samples! This user-friendly activity is great for all ages and abilities. The parking is plentiful and it's an easy flat walk around the coffee plantation for a short, free, self-guided tour. Additionally, free guided tours are also available at 10:00am, 12:00pm, 2:00pm, and 4:00pm. We enjoyed reading plaques to understand the history of the Kaua'i Coffee Plantation and looking at how the coffee beans are grown and harvested.

After your short walk around the plantation, the air-conditioned store tempts you with unique t-shirts, crafts and other branded souvenirs, in addition to the expected bags of coffee for sale. One of my most treasured and unusual mementos from the island was purchased at this store. They sell the actual burlap bags that coffee beans come in for your creative use. They're inexpensive and unusual. Every year the custom-imprinted business logo changes, so your burlap bag is essentially a piece of art. Mine is framed and hung on the wall of our mainland home for year-round enjoyment.

Now for the sampling! A variety of hot flavored coffees are available for your unlimited sampling. Small shot-glass sized cups are provided at no charge. (Incidentally, these small cups also make for a complimentary souvenir to take home!) For a quarter, you can purchase a small cup of cream to add to your coffee samples, and sugar/sweeteners are offered at no charge. This is a fun way to explore unusual coffee combinations that you might never try at home, so be adventurous!

The second complimentary sample is at the inside cash register where your sampling is closely monitored of candied coffee beans -- available for you to try at no charge.

Before you leave, check out the souvenir penny machine in the courtyard. For $.51, you can create your own keepsake memento. My children enjoy collecting these from all of our vacations as they don't break the bank!

Kaua'i's Hindu Monastery

Saiva Siddhanta Church Headquarters

107 Kaholalele Rd, Kapaa

808-822-3012

A free activity with ample parking. A peaceful oasis! The Hindu Monastery graciously allows access to a portion of its grounds Monday - Friday from 9:00am – 12:00pm. You're not allowed to go anywhere near the new temple, which is under construction and looks amazing, but the existing worship space is open. They're quite strict about visiting hours,

so pay close attention to that - a phone call to double check when visitors are allowed is probably a good idea. There is a worship service (all are welcomed) from 9:00am to 10:45am and the grounds are open for viewing from 10:45 to noon. Respectful dress code enforced: no shorts, tank tops, or bare legs for men or women (sarongs are provided to wear during your visit at no charge). Be prepared to remove your shoes before entering the temple area.

The grounds, which are open to the public, are small but stunning. If you have ever marveled at the Banyan trees featured during the movie, Jurassic Park, you will be excited to explore the grounds. Touching a real Banyan tree makes the drive to the Hindu Monetary entirely worthwhile!

Here, you are able to walk inside an enormous banyan tree to discover a huge black three-headed statue. Marvel at the 16-ton statue of a black bull which faces the entrance of the temple. Inside the temple you can observe, in silence, 108 statues of the god Siva performing his celestial dance. Also, you will be mesmerized by an amazing stone and

crystal artifact which depicts the movement of the planets and stars. Finally, Lord Siva in the central altar, sits as a focal point, flanked by two other deities.

Don't forget to pass through the gift shop for a look at some really special souvenirs that you will not find anywhere else on the island.

Waimea Canyon

Waimea Canyon Dr, Waimea

The Waimea Canyon is advertised as the number one tourist draw on Kaua'i. It's a free adventure, so of course we recommend you scheduling this drive during one full day of your vacation. Be prepared for a long drive, however, and potential car sickness due to the winding roads. With gorgeous views, this exhausting trip is one of those adventures that make you want to do it all over again on your next trip to Kaua'i. Pack your binoculars, saltines, and bag of snacks and get ready to see the Grand Canyon of the islands.

When we drove up the long winding road to the canyon, we thought it might never end. If you have small children with you, plan ahead with activities to keep them entertained during the long car ride. There are two options to access the canyon. We recommend driving directly to the canyon from Waimea on the 550; this road is much nicer than the Kokee Road (on your way home, you can take the alternative route down Kokee Road).

Some "must see" stops in your journey include:

> Waimea Canyon Lookout, between mile marker 10 and 11 on Waimea Canyon Road
> Puu Hina Hina Lookout, between mile markers 13 and 14
> Kalalau Lookout, Two miles above Kokee
> Pu'u O Kila Lookout
> Cliff Trail Lookout (0.8 mile on foot / 20 minutes one way)

There is a two-level lookout at the Waimea Canyon lookout, the lower one is easily accessible but the upper one requires a walk up a single set of stairs. It has a gentle incline cement sidewalk to get up there, even a wheelchair could make it. It can be breezy, damp, or even cold – so dress accordingly. The views are spectacular, simply stunning! At the bottom of the walkway, there was a family vendor selling local produce and homemade desserts on the edge of the parking lot. We purchased the diced mango, papaya and other local fruits we have never seen before.

The Waimea Canyon is "one of the wettest spots on earth," so rain and low cloud are common.

Stop at the overlooks and take lots of pics. Take a picnic lunch if you can to avoid having to pay for lunch at the one and only restaurant available. The little Lodge restaurant serves a limited menu with few tables. Be warned that on the last two trips that we made into the canyon, we were so hungry by midday that we stopped at this restaurant. It was busy with other hungry families and the service was overwhelmed (polite way of saying poor service), which we suspect is the norm. Pack your own lunch or return to Waimea for a meal instead.

The gift shop inside the restaurant sells some unique items not found elsewhere. Check out the museum for a great display of native and non-native plants and animals. The museum is free and open daily 10-4.

Waimea Canyon offers a plethora of short and long-distance hikes for all skill levels. If you are an avid hiker, we recommend your using the park's official guide to plan a wilderness excursion. We haven't put these hikes at the top of our recommendation list

for a few reasons -- getting to the canyon in and of itself usually eats up most of a day, not leaving much time left over for a serious hike. That being said, we acknowledge that many opportunities for amazing hikes at the Waimea Canyon are undiscovered from our family.

City of Waimea

On your way to visit the Waimea Canyon, you will probably pass through the town of Waimea. This is the best place for a final restroom break as well as a meal since you will most probably be famished after the several hours you spent exploring the canyon.

West Kaua'i Technology & Visitor Center is a hidden gem that is totally free and well worth your time. This is a great place to stop along the way to Waimea Canyon. There is a small museum with displays about the history of Koloa Town. They offer free guided walks through the town of Waimea with a local guide. There is no admission fee. Advance reservations are required due to the limited spots available for the tour, a three hour nonstop walk from 9-12 on Mondays. The tour stops along many historical sites in town.

The Aloha Friday Lei Making class offered at the West Kaua'i Technology and Visitor Center was also very nice as there was an assortment of different types of flowers used to make our leis- not just the usual plumeria – even bougainvillea and stephanotis flowers available. It was a great combination of flowers- so full of color. Free computer use is available on the premises. A great air-conditioned place for a short break from a long drive. The museum is also very nice with exhibits of the Waimea historical sites along with pictures and examples. There are also a lot of books sold here as well as the famous rare Niihau shell necklaces. There are a few computers for visitors to utilize which is very convenient. Definitely worthwhile to stop by here and at least say "hi." By the way, everything here was free but donations are greatly accepted to keep the program running.

There are not many choices when it comes to a quick lunch in Waimea and as far as we can tell, none of them are inexpensive. The two most popular tourist restaurants in town are Island Taco and Shrimp Station. Both were packed the last time we were in town and the prices were enough to make us just hold off and wait another half hour and eat lunch in Poipu.

As for a special desert that just screams "Kaua'i Cuisine", you must try Aunty Liliko'i. You want Lilikoi flavor (yellow passion fruit)? Well, they have it all. My personal favorites are the Lilikoi mustards. They are just terrifically spicy and sweet. The staff is phenomenal and willing to let you try many samples. On the way to Waimea Canyon, the shop sits just off the main road. Another great option is you can get a slice of Lilikoi Chiffon Pie or Lilikoi Fudge! There is a wide selection of sauces & juice, and you can get it gift boxed with a reusable tote. If you are driving to Waimea Canyon, be sure to stop at Aunty Lilikoi's for dessert on the way back.

The Giant Aloha Shirt

Waimea Canyon General Store

8171 Kekaha Rd, Kekaha

The giant aloha shirt makes for a fun stop on your drive up to the canyon. This souvenir shop may not offer the best prices, but it makes up for it with charm and unique items for sale. The biggest draw is the giant aloha shirt displayed outside, sized 28XL if you can believe that. What a terrific photo op!

Spouting Horn

Lawai Rd., Koloa

This is a very popular attraction on the south side of Kaua'i. Just a few miles from Poipu, we visit the Spouting Horn on every visit to Kaua'i because it is free, convenient and spectacular! This natural phenomenon is caused from the strong waves being drawn into lava tubes. The air is somehow trapped, shooting high in the sky through a chimney-like hole. The water show is consistently impressive like the Bellagio fountains, and operates 24/7. The spout can be seen from many of the oceanfront hotels and condos all the way in Poipu.

There is a large craft fair/souvenir bazaar onsite that is just as attractive. About a dozen booths line the sidewalk as you walk from your car to the spouting horn. But beware! We have learned from frequent visits to the Spouting Horn bazaar that the majority of these souvenirs are duplicates of those being sold at cheaper locations on the island like Kmart, Wal-Mart, or the ABC Store for a fraction of the cost.

Parking is easy and plentiful, and public bathrooms are available. This is a great activity for all ages and is user-friendly (strollers, wheel-chairs, etc.).

The Tree Tunnel

Highway 520 toward Poipu

My absolute favorite drive on Kaua'i is the magnificent mile of magical trees along highway 520 toward Poipu. These overgrown eucalyptus trees create a cavernous effect for the two-lane road, which is nothing short of magical.

The tunnel of trees was created by the legacy of Walter Duncan McBryde who had more than 500 trees leftover when he landscaped his estate! The trees have survived more than 150 years, coming back stronger than ever after tropical storms or hurricanes.

There isn't a safe place to pull over for photos so you will have to rely on your vehicle passengers to document the memory of driving into this fairytale tunnel.

The ultimate experience would be to participate in Kaua'i's annual marathon where runners can experience the treetop glory first-hand on foot, held every September.

Hula Dancing Shows

Maybe paying over a hundred dollars per person to watch hula dancers at a luau isn't your cup of poi. We would have to agree! But enjoying the art of the hula (not to mention the beautiful Polynesian costumes) must be at the top of your list for a complete Hawaiian vacation.

FREE hula performances are offered to the public in multiple venues. Schedules may change, so be sure to call ahead for any updates.

Poipu Shopping Village – Tahitian and Hula, Thursdays 5:00pm

808.742.2831

Suggestion: Pair this experience with dinner at Keoki's Paradise, eating in the bar area for substantial discounts, of course!

Harbor Mall, Lihue – Hawaiian entertainment and hula, Wednesday's 12:15pm

808.245.6255

Coconut Marketplace, Wailua – Hula show, Wednesdays 5:00pm, Saturdays 1:00pm

808.822.3641

Grand Hyatt Kaua'i – Sea View Terrace, Torch Lighting Ceremony Tuesday, Friday, Saturday from 6:15; Entertainment and hula every evening 5-8

808.742.1234

Five Star Hotels: Pool/Beaches

Just because you aren't staying at a five-star resort doesn't mean you can't take a peek at how the other half lives. The major resorts on the island are situated on the most pristine beaches, and thanks to Hawaii Revised Statutes 115-5, 205A-1, the public must be granted access.

Each resort offers a small public parking lot and path to the public beach.

If you want the full movie-star experience without the outrageous tab, consider having a cocktail on location. You can enjoy the more convenient and plentiful resort guest parking, and strut through the lobby on a mission.

The St. Regis Princeville Resort, **5520 Ka Haku Rd., Princeville**

Grand Hyatt Kaua'i, **1571 Poipu Rd., Poipu**

Ko'a Kea Hotel and Resort, **2251 Poipu Rd., Koloa**

The Westin Princeville Ocean Resort Villas, **3838 Wyllie Rd., Princeville**

Marriott Kaua'i Lagoons/**Kalanipu'u, 3325 Holokawelu Way, Poipu**

Sheraton Kaua'i, **2440 Hoonani Rd., Poipu**

Hanalei Colony Resort, **5-7130 Kuhio Hwy, Hanalei Bay**

Kaua'i Marriott, **3610 Rice St., Lihue**

Family portraits

You might think a family portrait is a weird way to kill an hour on your vacation, but I'm here to tell you that the memory lives on. I've looked into hiring a professional photographer, and the costs are pretty outrageous. Your iPad or iPhone will do just fine! So, get dressed, find a shady spot, and grab a stranger.

Speaking as someone who once-upon-a-time worked as a photographer in Monterey, CA, I feel I know a thing or two and can provide some easy and free advice to help you along here. First, plan ahead. Back at home, make some decisions about what you'd like your family to wear. It can be as simple as all white shirts, but I recommend deciding on a unifying color palate to give your family portrait a professional look. Second, find a spot in the shade. Everyone looks more attractive without stark shadows caused by direct sunlight. Plus, no one will be squinting and you can remove your sunglasses without going blind. Lastly, since you're working with a digital camera, and there is no cost involved, plan on taking a million shots! Eventually, your family will agree on that one special pose to enlarge and hang on the wall.

A tip about aloha shirts — most people buy them in Hawaii for a pretty penny, but then toss them in the donation pile when they return home to the mainland. You can pick up these aloha shirts at your local thrift store back home for a few dollars each! Toss the shirts in the laundry and pack in your suitcase to enjoy on vacation. Your Facebook friends will be none the wiser.

Church Service

Waioli Huiia Church, Hanalei

Sundays at 10am English/Hawaiian free church service open to worshipers. This darling green church with roots from Christian missionaries was built in the style of American Gothic architecture. One might think it looks like a movie set with the distinct Hanalei cliffs as a backdrop. It might look like the church you are used to sitting in with pews and looking at the stained-glass windows around you, but when you glance at the parishioners wearing aloha shirts and flip flops (welcomed attire), you realize you are experiencing something unique to Hawaii. Expect a sermon dotted with Hawaiian words and phrases and enjoy!

"Aloha Kakahiaka" - Good Morning

"`Ohana" - family, extended family, clan, kin group

"E pule ka kou" - Let us pray

"Kahu" - pastor (literally means shepherd)

"Iesu" - Jesus

"Ke Akua" - God

"Ka Haku" - The Lord

"Keiki" - children

"Kuleana" - right, responsibility, authority

"Lokomaika`i" - good will, generosity, kindness, gracious

Luau Crashers

I'm going to anger a lot of locals in the next paragraph, and for that I am truly sorry. Yes, the tourists should help drive the Kaua'i economy, but to pay over a $100 a person to eat food cooked in the dirt while sitting on plastic chairs to watch a performance? Perhaps not! I would like to remind the readers that all the beaches are public land on Kaua'i. That means, if you just HAPPEN to be camped out on the beach when a luau begins at a fabulous five-star hotel, you are legally allowed to sit on the towel you brought (not the hotel-owned beach chairs), and enjoy watching the performance. I am not encouraging actually crashing the actual luau (although I'm sure some cheapskates have tried this!), I'm just pointing out the fact that the singers, dancers, and fire performances can be enjoyed for free from the beach, (albeit at a weird angle). The dates

and times of luaus are posted on the website of each hotel. Note the venue can change depending on weather, or even become cancelled, so it is best to confirm with the hotel prior to making the trip over there. The rest is up to you!

Additionally, when the luau ends, the custom is for the performers to stay afterwards and pose for photos. Obviously, it would be rude for you to cut in front of paying luau guests, but when the lines diminish, I have found the performers to be most gracious in posing for a quick snapshot.

Glass Beach

Waialo Rd., Port Allen

The location of the Glass Beach is not far from Hanapepe. There are no signs or posted directions for travelers, but Waialo Rd., Port Allen will help guide your GPS. Many boat tours depart from the docking area as well. The exact location is between the Asian Cemetery and Chevron oil refinery. Park along the dirt road and walk the windy path to the beach, stepping over dumped engines and other forgotten debris. This is an unattractive and hard to find location!

Sea glass is essentially created from trash dumped into the ocean or left on the beach. Over many years, the waves and salt water soften the texture of broken glass and will even change its composition from clear to opaque. What was once a beer bottle or broken windshield is dispersed into a million pieces and later washed ashore as beautiful small stones.

The glass is not as plentiful as it was in the past, so be patient with exploration. You are certain to bring home a handful that you will treasure forever. Your friends will delight in seeing your display of stones more than any made-in-China t-shirt, and the best part is that this souvenir is free.

The Japanese cemetery adjacent the glass beach is also interesting but for some reason not publicized and sadly, poorly maintained.

Kaua'i Kookie Factory

2-2436 Kaumualii Hwy, Kalaheo (storefront)

1-3529 Kaumualii Hwy, Hanapepe, hours 10-5 (Factory location with store)

This gem of a stop will cure your sweet tooth. Macadamia Nut Shortbread, Guava, Passion Fruit, and Papaya are just a few of the island flavored cookies and treats you will sample! Did I mention the samples are free? The restaurant and bakery will even tempt you with affordable breakfast or lunch plates. The dine-in option has a cozy diner feel and you won't leave hungry. We recommend you try a local's favorite, the Loco Moco: eggs, a hamburger patty, and rice. Your friends back home will appreciate a gift purchased here too. Another bonus is that these desserts are unique to Kaua'i, and not sold on the other islands.

Cave Exploration – Hanalei

5-7878 Kuhio Hwy, Hanalei

Are you a spelunker? Before deciding to explore a cave on Kauaʻi, read the posted signs. Some caves are unstable or unavailable to the public. Falling rocks pose a real danger as does bacteria growing in the water (specifically, leptospirosis). When in doubt, follow the rules posted.

If you dare to enter the accessible and permitted caves, be sure to LOOK UP! Thousands of bats and spider webs coat the ceiling of the caves. Does this sound terrifying? You can stand at the entrance to the cave for a snapshot; your Facebook friends won't be able to tell the difference!

Maniniholo Dry Cave

5-7878 Kuhio Hwy, Hanalei

The Maniniholo Dry Cave is located at 5-7878 Kuhio Hwy and is the most accessible cave in Kaua'i. This natural wonder is easy to access and free for all ages to enjoy.

Ha'ena Beach Park is across the street with convenient parking lot (though limited spots) and even has public bathrooms.

Waikanaloa Cave and Waikapale Cave

Further past the Ha'ena public beach is the Waikanaloa Cave and Waikapale Cave. These wet caves (as in filled with water) are accessible via a short hike on the left side of the road past Ha'ena Beach. The uphill hike leads you toward the series of caves, the "Blue Room" being the last of the three. The more athletic and adventurous will appreciate the beauty of these spring-water filled caves, though swimming is not recommended. Does the Waikanaloa Cave look familiar? It was used in the filming of Pirates of the Caribbean on Stranger Tides. It's also known as the "Blue Room" as the cave glows with a striking blue light. Perhaps this is from the sun's reflection on calcite, or perhaps something more magical?

Hanalei Pier

The Hanalei Pier offers a truly iconic view of the sea and mountains coming together in a symphony of color and decadence. The sunsets are magnificent and the beach is large and relatively uncrowded. You may even see kids jumping off the pier. Parking is easy and the 1.8 mile walk or run from one end of the beach to the other beats a treadmill anytime. You might recognize the pier as filmed in the movie, "Soul Surfer," a fun movie to watch on the plane ride home.

Lei-Making

I totally stumbled upon the lei-making craft several years ago, and since then it has become a yearly favorite of my family. This simple craft can be accomplished by anyone in your group that is able to pinch a needle and thread. It's totally free and the finished product smells fantastic. Of course, your family will even want to wear them to dinner or even a family portrait?

In your suitcase, pack a small Tupperware with hearty thread (or thick twine), Scotch tape, several wide-eyed needles, and kid scissors. I like to check this in my luggage to prevent Homeland Security from investigating my bikinis.

Plumeria trees are rampant on the island, in public settings and around your condo or hotel. The constant island trade winds cause the flowers to drop to the ground, day in and day out. Put your loved ones to work by picking up all of the unbruised blooms in a plastic bag and head back to your hotel for an activity that is sure to delight each participant.

Knot your thread or string and secure with a large hunk of tape, and punch your needle through each flower as you might string popcorn for a Christmas tree. Try alternating bloom colors or string all the same, and soon you will have a delicate, free, custom lei to wear and enjoy on your vacation.

Leis usually don't last more than an evening, so if you hope to preserve your work of art, try putting it in the refrigerator to extend its life.

CHAPTER 6: Water & Land Sports

Boogie boarding

f you haven't tried boogie boarding, you're in for a thrill! Easier than surfing, boogie boarding means riding the waves using a short, rectangular foam board. Attach your board to the ankle or wrist and have fun! These boards are inexpensive and available at Kmart or Walmart at a decent price. Or, if you are lucky, catch a family leaving the island and they might "donate" their boards to you for free (this has happened to us many times-of course, we do the same when we leave).

Inner Tubes

Purchasing these delightful pool and ocean toys on the island might set you back a pretty penny. I beg you not to purchase these pricey items (or gasp, rent!) from your pricey hotel. The same tubes are for sale at your local Wal-Mart back home. Buy it on sale, pack in your suitcase, and enjoy! The same goes for beach balls, arm floaties, and other rafts. No matter what your age is, everyone enjoys floating in the warm ocean without a care in the world.

Surfing and SUP (Stand Up Paddleboarding)

Have you ever dreamed of learning to surf? You might be tempted by the allure of the strapping young men under the umbrella stations advertising lessons. For upwards of hundreds of dollars, you can have an hour of private one/one instruction, or for a bit less, commit to small group instruction. Surfing requires a strong swimming base and a comfort level in the ocean.

Many brave readers will want to bypass the shenanigans and showboating of paying for surfing instructions and give surfing a try on their own. We have had great luck buying surf boards at local thrift shops to use during our stay, for a fraction of the rental cost. Additionally, it's not hard to find good surfing spots on the island. They're everywhere!

Be honest with yourself about what you can handle. Be observant of the skill level you see among the surfers. If the crowd looks like a bunch of rookies with an instructor, this might be a good place to start surfing! Many public beaches in Kaua'i also post beach lifeguards. This would also be a good place to start in case you run into trouble.

SUP or Stand Up Paddleboarding is less expensive for rental purposes and much safer for the ocean novice.

Land Sports

Surprisingly, there comes a point in the vacation where everyone is just a bit tired of the water. I know, I know, how is that possible? I have found that packing a kite and maybe even a blow-up ball in my suitcase helps to kill the time on those off-days when folks need a break.

If golf or bike riding tickles your fancy, check out the suggestions further on in the next section: Bargain Activities.

Beach Activities

The sand of Kaua'i is like no other. So soft and luxurious! You may want to invest in those roll up grass matts if your resort doesn't offer beach chairs to sit on. These are available at Kmart or Walmart for just a few dollars. The sand shakes right off them and they never get too hot to sit on.

In our early visits to Kaua'i, we would purchase disposable underwater cameras (did we just date ourselves or what?). Nowadays, a GO-PRO Hero (earliest version because yes, we are that cheap) can be purchased for less than a hundred dollars on eBay and will provide your family hours of fun taking underwater photos, beach shots, and action videos. The best part is that you never run out of film and don't have to worry about sand/water ruining your camera or phone. Be sure to attach the floaty to your camera so it doesn't sink!

All of the beaches in Kaua'i are worth exploring, but we wanted to highlight a few of our favorites that offer a unique experience.

Kee Beach

Kee Beach, Hanalei - Near the trailhead for Kalalau Trail. This amazing jewel of a beach offers the worst parking, but one of the best snorkeling experiences on the island. It's great for kids (gentle waves), has lifeguards on duty, and offers those stunning Napali Coast lush mountains as your vista as you float in the water. Amazing! There is a crowded public bathroom available for changing clothes, and an outdoor shower area to rinse off your boogie boards and sandals. However, there is NO FOOD OR DRINKS for sale anywhere close to this location, so please plan ahead. (Suggestion: Stop in Hanalei Bay at Bubba's on your way in or out to this beach.)

Lydgate Beach Park
Nalu Road Uninc. Kaua'i County Hawaii, Kapaa

Lydgate Beach Park, is a public beach enjoyed by droves of locals. This large public park offers ample public restrooms to change in and even shaded and covered picnic table areas to enjoy lunch. There is ample parking and the location is easy to get to near the Lihue airport on your way to Kapaa. We like this beach for beginning snorkeling and/or for young children as there is a very protected, shallow area in the ocean bordered by a wall of lava rocks. For those of you trying to learn a few things, a giant poster of all of the Hawaiian fish is posted on the path for your reference. Lifeguards on duty.

Kalapaki Beach

Kalapaki Beach, Lihue is one of my favorite protected beaches in Lihue next to the Marriott Beach Club. This beach offers gentle waves thanks to the breakers sheltering the cove. Cruise ships dock in this area, and gorgeous multimillion dollar homes dot the cliffs looking down. You can access this beach via the public access lot through the Marriott property. Duke's Canoe Club restaurant is on site, and is a favorite bar-style restaurant for our family. The prices are "island reasonable" and they have a lively bar area. We have an expensive tradition of ordering a drink served inside a pineapple here. The empty pineapple lives on in our refrigerator for the rest of the trip, being refilled and celebrated!

A short walk along Kalapaki Beach takes you to the Kalapaki Beach Hut which offers a delicious low-cost hearty breakfast among other casual walk-up style entrees.

When all else fails, the ABC Store at Kalapaki Beach is one of your least-expensive options to purchase souvenirs, beverages or snacks, and the prices are far less than those offered at the neighboring resort gift shops.

Poipu Beach Park

Poipu Beach Park, Poipu/Koloa is by far our first choice for beaches on the island. This beach tends to be sunny even when the rest of the island is drenched in rainfall. (Hint – add each section of the island to your weather app to plan each day's activities). Poipu

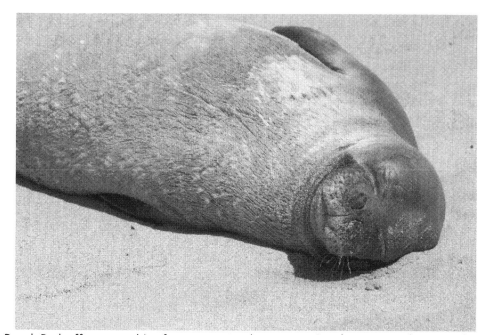

Beach Park offers something for everyone – the young enjoy the protected cove to chase sea turtles and bob in gentle waves under the watch of lifeguards and the more adventurous head out to deeper waters for surfing. No matter what your age, everyone is enticed to explore the changes in tide; you are able to magically "walk on water" out to a patch of shallow land via a disappearing isthmus. To top off your experience at Poipu Beach Park, you are likely to stumble across an important visitor: a Hawaiian Monk Seal that hops onto shore for an afternoon nap!

Shipwreck Beach

Shipwreck Beach, Poipu - The public beach which fronts the gorgeous Grand Hyatt in Poipu is known by locals as Shipwreck Beach. Complying with state law, the public must have access to the Hyatt's impressive beach landscape. Shipwreck Beach is accessed from a short trail off the public parking area, located immediately after the hotel guest parking lots for the Grand Hyatt. Alternatively, you can walk to Shipwreck Beach from neighboring Poipu hotels/condos by following Pe'e Road to the Grand Hyatt.

While Shipwreck beach itself may appear unassuming, the waves can become overpowering. Surf competitions are even held here. Safety Warning: Be forewarned about the treacherous nature of the waves for swimming at this location! Brittney Spears and her entourage vacationed here recently, and she was plucked from the undertow by her body guards. The waves at Shipwreck Beach have knocked over many a tourist. This, combined with the large boulders that pepper the beach, can lead to deadly results. There are no lifeguards present, and the signage continuously warns visitors about the posed danger.

While surfing at Shipwreck Beach might not be on your radar, watching the adventurous souls jump into the water from the high cliff above might be enough to entertain you. During high tide, locals and fans of the Anne Heche/Harrison Ford movie, "Six Days, Seven Nights," perilously jump from the cliffs into the sea below. They only do this during high tide so DO NOT try this on your own if there are no locals present.

Barking Sands Beach/Polihale State Beach

Part of the Polihale State Park in *Kekaha* is the Barking Sands Beach which is not for the faint of heart. It is the western portion of Polihale Beach. Access is challenging, and your rental car and anxiety level may not cooperate! This remote beach can only be reached via an extremely wild ride on a dirt, pot-holed sugarcane road on the very western tip of the island. 4WD and hearty vehicles recommend!

So, what is a barking sand? Legend explains that the sand makes a noise much like the bark of a dog. The friction of the moving grains of dry sand resonate vibrations when moved.

Why is this beach so secret? Adjacent to the Barking Sands Beach is the Pacific Missile Range Facility of the US Navy. This is the world's largest instrumented, multi-dimensional testing and training missile range. Wow! No wonder the military chose this remote and wild location. For those of you that have a valid military ID, you can access the Pacific Missile Range Facility and enjoy the beaches there as well as their convenience store(PX), movie theater etc. They also have very reasonably priced beachfront housing that can be booked for short stays.

If you can survive the five miles of fear, traveling at best 10 mph, you will be rewarded with a view of the Hawaiian landscape like no other. Without a trace of civilization present at the Barking Sands Beach, you might imagine what life was like for the original Hawaiians. It's breathtaking! Even the mountain goats will look like relics of a different era.

With very little shade and few relief public toilets, come prepared with sunscreen, water, and needed supplies.

Enjoy this unique experience on land, pretty please, as the water conditions are treacherous. There are no lifeguards available. Do not misjudge the danger of the water.

Puu Poa Beach

5454 Ka Haku Rd, Princeville

Accessed via the St. Regis Hotel.

Beautiful public beach adjacent to the sophisticated St. Regis Hotel in Princeville. Monkey pod shade trees offer a bit of cover for you to sit and enjoy reading a book. What makes this beach special and unique is the backdrop of mountains across the bay. The water is calm without many waves making it great for kayaking. The bottom floor is quite rocky, however, so be careful or wear your water shoes to protect your feet. We have heard from more than one family (us included) about the treacherous and rocky shoreline. The beach looks fine but when you enter the water, there is a rocky shelf that

has large holes in it that one of my kids fell in and scraped up a knee. Either remain swimming and don't try to stand or do what we did and stay on the beach. The beach in Hanalei is right down the coast and much safer!!

Wildlife

The beauty of Kaua'i extends beyond the lush tropical landscape to the critters that roam the island. While the wild roosters and chickens can definitely be annoying, they make the island experience unique! Where else in the world can you enjoy a meal in a fancy restaurant and feel a pecking on your ankle from a wild chicken! (True story, my son screamed at the top of his lungs in surprise!) Wild boars run amok in the jungle, and can be seen mostly at dawn and dusk crossing the road in even suburban areas!. Searching for ocean beauties like the Hawaiian Monk Seal or sea turtles will surely capture your heart and provide hours of free entertainment for your family. Even though the monk seals may swim or beach themselves next to you, be sure to keep hands off (it's the law!). The wildlife of Kaua'i is bountiful and free for you to visually enjoy – no tickets or passes required!

Tropical Birds at the Grand Hyatt

1571 Poipu Rd., Poipu

Parrots and tropical birds chat with guests in the open-air corridors and lobby of the Grand Hyatt. No cages! Beautiful creatures that jabber and delight on-lookers of all ages.

Keep walking throughout the gardens in the center lobby as multiple birds are stationed throughout. You can also ask hotel staff if any "bird presentations" will happen during your visit to the property. You can ask questions and learn from an informal and free presentation.

Also, be sure to check the "Great for Kids" section which includes fish feeding.

CHAPTER 7: Bargain Activities

T he following activities are not free, but low enough cost per person to be "worth the expense," and therefore recommended by Kaua'i Cheap Vacations.

Canoe/Kayak Rental and hike to the "Secret Waterfall"

Kamokila Hawaiian Village

Multiple businesses rent kayaks and/or canoes for you to explore the Wailua River, starting in Kapa'a. Some businesses offer a guide or even a package with lunch. We recommend saving wads of cash by packing your own lunch and just renting the boats solo. There are so many tourists out on the water, you won't have any difficulty finding your way to the designated tourist spots: Fern Grotto, hike to Secret Falls, and the rope swing.

Be sure to wear water shoes for this experience. You will be launching your boat in shallow water and your feet will be submerged. The river floor is muddy, slippery, and rocky, so shoes are a must. If you didn't pack water shoes, make a trip to Walmart or a thrift store prior to your river exploration so you come prepared. Additionally, you may want to bring bug spray and a water proof bag for phones/cameras. Pack plenty of water/snacks as you are venturing into the jungle without any restaurants or support.

Do not be intimidated by this activity. It's truly the highlight of our vacation! Even young children can participate by pairing them with a capable adult in the boat. Or, consider a canoe rental where a child can sit in the middle seat while adults steer and paddle (3 to a boat).

A few tips to make this a positive experience. Start early! The winds can pick up in the afternoon making it more challenging to paddle your course. Also, there are less

people on the river in the morning hours. Tour groups do not operate on Sundays on the river as it is reserved for locals.

While you have many companies to choose from, we like the "no frills" approach of the Kamokila Hawaiian Village. This locally owned landmark was even used during the filming of the movie "Outbreak". In addition to boat rentals, the site sells tickets to their cultural village tours, educational and fun to see the roaming peacocks. Remember to use their restroom before you paddle off as there are none up the river, except at the Fern Grotto. This walk to the restroom will give you a quick and free look at the preserved Hawaiian Village. Launching your canoe or kayak from this location starts you much further up the river, saving your arms some paddling time. They will provide you with a water-resistant bag for your personal items and a very simple map. Again, follow the crowds and enjoy your adventure!

The hike to the secret waterfall is about a mile from where you park your boat. The terrain is mostly flat, but technical, meaning lots of rocks/ground cover to navigate. There is even a shallow stream to cross while holding onto a tow rope. My children enjoyed this hike above all others. What more of an incentive do you need for a hike than to end up at a waterfall! And one you can swim under at that. Note there are no bathrooms, so wear your swim suit under your clothes and **bring old tennis shoes or water shoes!**

Fern Grotto

Access via canoe or kayak rental (see above) on the Wailua River-<u>cheapest option!</u>

Smith's Boat Tours

The Fern Grotto is known as the "most romantic spot on Kaua'i". It's a fern covered lava rock grotto that forms a natural amphitheater. When I was a child, visitors could explore the grotto walls directly, but hurricane damage over time changed the access for safety reasons. The grotto can now be enjoyed only from the observation deck.

If you are interested in a relaxed slow afternoon, we recommend taking one of the Smith boat tours. Elderly and young alike will enjoy a restful trip up the Wailua River while being serenaded with local folk musicians. The cost is under $20 per person and makes for a leisurely afternoon.

Bathrooms and hand railings will support your experience. Yes, this is somewhat of a "touristy" or cheesy destination, but nonetheless, one my entire family has repeatedly enjoyed.

Of course, the young and adventurous types will notice the kayakers and canoe paddlers headed toward the same destination (details included in previous segment). We have enjoyed both opportunities and highly recommend the Fern Grotto makes your list, no matter how you get there!

Kapa'a Biking

Coconut Bike Rental

Renting bikes is one of the lowest cost "big ticket" activities on the island. It is low-stress and enjoyable for all ages. Even the littlest keikis can be pulled along in bike trailers.

While there are many businesses offering bike rentals to tourists, our favorite is the **Coconut Bike Rental in Kapaa.** At the time of publication, they offered a YELP check-in deal with a discount for guests.

We have rented bikes from them several times, and found their customer service to be exceptional. Additionally, they offer a variety of bike options and accessories. Choices included BMX, beach cruisers, and mountain bikes for children and adults. Helmets were included for free, and all of the equipment was in excellent working condition.

For a small charge, you can add a basket to your bike rental. This is highly recommended as a convenient way to store your belongings. Of course, to save on expenses for the day, you must pack cold drinks and snacks from your hotel/condo! It's a bit windy, so be sure to bring a light jacket.

Along the shore of Kapaa is a public paved bike path. It is about 9 miles long, and covers easy to navigate terrain. There are public restrooms and water fountains along the path, and plenty of places to stop and rest. We recommend selecting the northern 4-mile segment toward Anahola, as the homeless tend to congregate on the opposite direction.

Our favorite stop along the ride is the "Pineapple Dump".

Up until the 1960s a pineapple manufacturer in nearby Kapaa loaded up left-over pineapple pieces (like skins and tops) onto carts, and dumped them off the end of this pier into the ocean! While you can't walk out onto the pier, it's an interesting photo op along your route.

If you still have time left on your rental, consider heading over to the ABC store for ice cream. It's just a couple of blocks from the bike rental store. Or, if you are famished, you might get a kick out of "Chicken in a Barrel," a restaurant where your meal is actually smoked in metal barrels in the restaurant's front yard!

St. Regis "Drinks by the Pool"

Nalu Kai Poolside Grill

St. Regis, Princeville

The St Regis Princeville boasts sophistication and elegance along the most beautiful coastline in Kaua'i. With a backdrop of Hanalei Bay, you won't see a better view unless sitting on the bow of a boat cruising along the Napali Coastline.

You don't have to pay $1,000 a night to enjoy the five-star luxury treatment this destination offers. Guests of the St Regis Princeville restaurants and bars will also receive the same movie star treatment!

Enjoy a $16 tropical cocktail or lunch entrée for around $20 at the Nalu Kai Poolside Grill and Bar, and snap a selfie. While this may seem like an outrageous sum for a cheapskate, keep in mind your bar tab is paying for the experience of enjoying the ambiance; You are truly a baller on a budget!

Lunch "With a Movie Star"

Tahiti Nui

5-5134 Kuhio Hwy, Hanalei

Enjoy lunch at the same restaurant where George Clooney dined in a scene from the movie "The Descendants". Or, pop in for a free photo at the bar!

Kukuiolono Golf Course

854 Puu Road, Kalaheo

Kukuiolono Golf Course is a lovely 9-hole golf course originally opened in 1928. The green fees can't be beat, between $7-$9, and each hole offers two difficulty levels. They have many sets of clubs available for rent as well as both pull and drive carts. You will be very surprised with the quality of golf you get for this very low price!

Take a leisurely stroll over the golf course and enjoy the spectacular views. The golf course is well kept and offers three little gems you should definitely take a look at during your game:

There is a pavilion located at the southern end of the golf course with great views. You can rent it for private events.

Enjoy the Japanese garden located almost at the center of the golf course.

Lastly, there is a rock garden with beautiful plants and Hawaiian artifacts and a small gazebo.

An interesting fact about this property is that it was donated by the McBryde family. You may recall this same family also donated the trees lining the "tree tunnel" heading toward Poipu.

Kilauea Lighthouse

Kilauea Road, Kilauea

808-828-1413

If you would like to learn about the birds of Kaua'i, this is a great place to start. For five dollars, you get to stroll along the pathway and learn about the various birds and see some beautiful scenery. On the way to Hanalei or Princeville, you can enjoy a stopover at this beautiful National Park. If you have an annual pass to National Parks, be sure to bring it with you. Outstanding views of the coastline here, and if you are lucky, you will even spot some whales traveling by. Tip: Folks with a disabled placard or current/retired military are free at all National Parks.

The historic lighthouse is situated on a point and offers beautiful views of the coast and ocean. During business hours, there is a building open with information about the lighthouse and wildlife. Tours may be available during your visit, so be sure to inquire at the time of your arrival to get on "the list".

Binoculars are complimentary. Be sure to check out the educational indoor exhibit to learn more about the history and wildlife. Clean bathrooms available. This activity is easily accessible and enjoyable for all ages.

Race Day!

This might sound counterintuitive to a relaxing Hawaiian vacation, but participating in a local race (5K or even the Kauai Marathon!) can be a great experience for the whole family. Google your vacation dates along with Kauai 5K or run to see if your dates match up to any scheduled events. We were surprised how much fun this event was for us! The minimal cost even included custom tank tops, swag, and snacks afterward.

CHAPTER 8: Great for Kids!

W e believe everything about Kaua'i can be enjoyed by your entire family. This is a family destination with wholesome and safe activities for all. That being said, we would have to say that certain activities might be *especially enjoyed* by the little ones in your group.

SPCA

3-825 Kaumualii Hwy in Lihue

Do you miss your dog while on vacation? If you're like us, we usually bring our dog along on trips. She is part of our family! We even have the kennel take photos of our dog and email them to us while we are in Kaua'i.

We found a way to get your "dog fix" while visiting the island. The best part is that its FREE and will make you feel good about yourself (unlike that Hula Pie you ate for dessert last night).

Basically, the SPCA lets you borrow a well-behaved kennel guest for a field trip of your own design. This helps the dogs get exercise, love and socialization while they wait to be permanently adopted.

We recommend arriving early on your field trip day so you have "pick of the litter" (if that is important to you.) You will fill out some paperwork at the front desk, then be permitted to walk through the kennels to select a match. These dogs have been screened by the staff as safe animals that will (hopefully) behave on your adventure. After you make your selection, the SPCA will hand you a leash, bag of treats, and a water bowl. Your buddy is then dressed in a cute vest that says "Adopt me!" Be prepared to make friends everywhere you go! Even local residents of Kaua'i participate in the fun.

Of course, the danger here is that you may fall in love with your new friend. The SPCA is prepared to help you permanently adopt your animal and will even help you coordinate travel home on the plane.

Additionally, if you happen to be flying on Alaska Airlines, the SPCA is always looking for volunteers to help assist already-adopted animals to fly back to the mainland. This is a free (unpaid) service on behalf of Alaska Airlines, and a great help to the animal en route to his new home.

The SPCA of Kaua'i is located at 3-825 Kaumualii Hwy in Lihue. Pick up hours are 11am-1pm Tuesday-Friday and 10am-12pm Saturday and Monday, with returns by 530pm Tuesday-Friday, and 3:30pm Saturday and Monday.

Lydgate Park Snorkeling

Wailua, Kaua'i

Off Route 56 between Kapaa and Lihue near the Wailua River Bridge

Lydgate Beach Park – Public beach enjoyed by local residents. Offers simple public restrooms to change in and some shaded covered picnic tabled areas to enjoy a picnic. Ample parking and easy to get to near the Lihue airport en-route to Kapaa. We like this beach for beginning snorkeling and for young children as there is a very protected, shallow area for snorkeling. There is even a giant playground for the little ones to burn off extra energy! For those of you trying to learn a few things, a giant poster of all of the Hawaiian fish is posted on the path for your reference. Lifeguards on duty.

Fish Feeding

Grand Hyatt Kaua'i, 1571 Poipu Rd., Poipu

Kaua'i Marriott Resort, 3610 Rice Street, Lihue

Koi fill the ponds in the lobbies of both beautiful resorts. These brightly colored carp practically jump out of the water during feeding time. Resort staff distribute small cups of fish food for the guests to feed the well-stocked ponds. Fish feeding varies according to the resort, so be sure to call ahead about the time it is scheduled during your stay. Free and occurs daily.

Kaua'i Plantation Railway

3-2087 Kaumualii Highway, Lihue (next to Kaua'i Community College)

All aboard! Explore 100 acres of Kaua'i agriculture on a short train trip that lasts about an hour. You will learn about Kaua'i's history and see firsthand how 50 varieties of crops like sugar, pineapple, banana, papaya and coffee are grown. This working farm also has animals like pigs, goats, sheep, cattle and horses. When most activities in Kaua'i hover over the hundred-dollar mark, this historic plantation railway experience is less than $20 per person. Additionally, the site of this experience is located at the beautiful Kilohana Plantation mansion.

CHAPTER 9: Dining Out

Plate Lunches

F ruit and sugar plantations from the 1880s fed plantation workers on-site. The laborers were served a single plate for lunch, usually scoops of rice with meat. Some suspect the origins of the plate lunch traces back to the traditional bento box, as many of the plantation workers emigrated from Asian countries. Over time, the rice and meat plate was expanded to include macaroni salad.

Throughout the island, you will see "plate lunch" advertised. This has become a Hawaiian tradition at hole-in-the-wall and upscale restaurants alike!

Some of our favorite plate lunches can be found at any of the Foodland or Times Supermarket stores or restaurants like "Marks Place" in Lihue. My personal favorite is in the parking lot of Suki's Market in Koloa.

"Cheap Eats" with Local Style

Bubbas

Bubbas has three locations: Kapaa, Hanalei, Poipu

Bubba's Burger is my son's favorite restaurant on the island. Not only is his nickname 'Bubba" but his favorite food is cheeseburgers. This walk-up style restaurant is quick and relatively inexpensive, but much tastier than fast food.

The menu is simple and offers the basic kids-appetite $4.00 1/6 lb. Bubba Burger all he way up to a Double Slopper ½ lb. with chili for close to $10.00. Corn dogs, onion rings, and Caesar salads round out the menu.

Lines can be long during the lunch hour, so include your wait time in your planning. As my husband likes to say, "if folks in line are wearing neon colored-construction uniforms (as in maintenance or construction labor), the restaurant is enjoyed by local residents therefore must be a good deal!" (meaning – local residents know where the good deals are and likely not paying high-priced tourist dollars).

While you wait for your order to be called, peruse the walls of Bubba's for a stroll down the hall of fame. It seems every movie star ever to visit Kaua'i has had their photo taken at this restaurant.

Insider's Tip – If you wear any item of clothing (hat, shirt, shorts etc.) printed with the Bubba's logo, you receive your soda (and refills!) for free. This includes current and past designs, so check your thrift stores carefully!

Da Crack

2827 Poipu Rd, Koloa

Every time we vacation in Kaua'i we come to Da Crack! The name and location will make you wonder if you are at the right place but **just be patient, you WILL NOT be let down!!** The prices are reasonable and the service is quick and friendly. Portions are large, and of course the quality and taste is excellent. We order the bowls (burrito without the tortilla) and enjoy leftovers for dinner. Highly recommend this lunch spot – don't judge it by its appearance. Also, don't be surprised by the use of thinly shredded cabbage in place of the lettuce. This is due to the complexities of sourcing lettuce on the island (cost) but don't despair, you won't really notice!

Do not plan on wait staff or even a table to sit and eat at. This walk up counter best serves "to go". Otherwise, you will be fighting to sit and eat with your lap as a table or

the single park bench out front. Parking is very limited and the lines are long over the lunch hour so plan accordingly.

Kalapaki Beach Hut

3474 Rice St, Lihue

The Kalapaki Beach Hut is a fun little spot for a quick breakfast or lunch. You can dine up on the second level if available. This is an excellent alternative to all the outrageously priced food in the Kalapaki Beach area. Dependable comfort food: burgers, pork sandwich etc. shaved ice also. If you see a local residents dining at the restaurant you chose, then you can guess that it's affordable and quality food! This is where I learned what POG drink stood for- Pineapple, Orange and Guava juice and the loco moco: white rice, topped with a hamburger patty, a fried egg, and brown gravy. Yum!

CHAPTER 10: DINING OUT - Bars & Bar Menus

Bars

Be forwarded that the entire island of Kaua'i is quite sleepy after sundown! This is not the vacation spot for those used to the fast-paced nightlife of Las Vegas. That said, there is always a bar serving cold drinks and welcoming new friends. After all, you are on vacation!

By no means is this an exhaustive list of bars and nightlife. Kaua'i Cheap Vacations recommends you buy your own alcohol at a local grocery store to save money! We will recommend a few spots, however, just in case:

Bars OPEN LATE!

Rob's Good Time Grill **(11:00am-2:00am)**

4303 Rice St, Rice Shopping Ctr., Lihue

Happy hour, trivia, karaoke, DJ dancing

Celebrated the night away here on a big milestone birthday, I must share!

Bars with LIVE MUSIC

Duke's Kaua'i

3610 Rice St, Lihue

Live music Monday, Wednesday, Thursday, Friday and Sunday 4:00-6:00pm

Friday and Saturday 8:30-10:30pm

Kalapaki Joes of Poipu

1941 Poipu Rd, Koloa

Live music every Saturday at 6:00pm

Brenneckee's Beach Broiler

2100 Hoone Road, Poipu Beach, Koloa

Thursday, Friday, Saturday 8:30-11:00pm

Rewards Programs (Birthday, Anniversary)

Keoki's Paradise

2360 Kiahuna Plantation Dr., Koloa

We have discovered that many restaurants in our travels offer a free entrée, appetizer, or even a dessert during the month of your registered special occasion (birthday, anniversary). If you plan on celebrating one such occasion during your vacation to Kaua'i, be sure to register online prior to your trip with Keoki's Paradise. They will send you an email with a voucher to redeem at the restaurant. Cool!

Bar Menu and Happy Hour Menus

Keoki's Paradise

2360 Kiahuna Plantation Dr., Koloa

Many upscale restaurants in Kaua'i offer a heavily discounted menu during "Aloha hour" or happy hour. You are able to enjoy the same food, prepared by the same chefs, and eaten by those tourists sitting in the main dining room at a fraction of the cost simply by eating in the bar area (same view/same outdoor seating).

For example, the current discounted menu at Keoki's Paradise in Poipu (subject to change):

Aloha Hour in the Bamboo Bar is from 3:00-5:00pm and 9:30-10:30pm

Beers from $5, Cocktails from $7, Wine from $6

Sliders $4, Prime Rib Bones $6, Tacos $4

Chef's Tasting Menu (Happy Hour) daily 4:45-5:30

An absolute must if you plan on splurging and want a complete meal in the main dining room! We go to Keoki's Paradise EVERY time we visit Kaua'i and we always eat dinner early and order off the Chef's Tasting menu if we want a fancy dinner. If dining between the above hours (in the Dining Room), please ask for this menu as they sometimes "forget" to include it when you are seated.

$26 gets you a starter, entree and dessert. Yes, that sounds pricey by mainland standards, but don't forget that this is world class island cuisine and worth every penny! A trick we learned is ask your waiter to "trade in" your two dessert picks for one slice of Hula Pie (not a listed option on the Chef's Tasting Menu) to share. So Yummy!

Duke's Kaua'i

3610 Rice St, Lihue

Taco Tuesdays from 4:00-6:00pm

Beers from $5

Kailua Pork Tacos $3.5, Fresh Fish Tacos $4.5

Brenneckee's Beach Broiler

2100 Hoone Road, Poipu Beach, Koloa

Happy Hour Pupu's and discounted drinks served daily from 3:00 to 5:00pm and 8:30 to 9:30.

CHAPTER 11: DINING OUT - Coupons, Fast Food

Travelzoo/Groupon

ften search engines like www.travelzoo.com pick up specials offered on meals in Kaua'i. An example of a discount participator is the Tortilla Republic, a sophisticated upscale Mexican restaurant in The Shops at Kukui'ula, 2829 Ala Kalanikumaka St. in Koloa.

Be sure to check www.Groupon.com also as they are constantly adding new offers for food or activities.

FAST FOOD

McDonalds

Not surprisingly, there are four McDonalds on the island of Kaua'i. Everyone thinks there are only three, but folks forget there is one hidden inside of Walmart in Lihue!

3113 Kuhio Hwy, Lihue; 3-3300 Kuhio Hwy, Lihue; 4-0771 Kuhio Hwy, Kapaa; and 4469 Waialo Rd, Eleele

You might feel like a failure as a tourist hitting a McDonalds while on the garden island, but alas, I have news that can save your conscience. McDonalds actually serve SOME flavors from the island! The breakfast menu includes an offering of SPAM! What is SPAM you ask? Leftover from the WWII era influence, SPAM is an island favorite. It's a brand of canned cooked meat (ham and pork) made by Hormel Foods Corporation. Hawaiians enjoy this "delicacy" in their sushi rolls or as a side dish, like with fried eggs and rice. Some even go so far as to call SPAM the "steak of Hawaii," as more than 7 million cans of SPAM are consumed each year in our 50th state!

Additionally, I have even seen desserts at McDonalds adopt unique island flavors. The pies sold in Kaua'i might not be the apple or cherry that you are used to back on the mainland. Coconut or taro (poi) flavored pie might be available, so indulge!

Over the years, McDonalds on the islands has offered a variety of unique menu items, such as the McTeri burger, saimin (Ramen type noodles) or fruit punch drink, so give something new a try. Make plans to include McDonalds as an inexpensive meal while on vacation without feeling like you are taking a short-cut.

Little Caesars

As we have learned above, dining out in Kaua'i on a budget is almost impossible. One of the few places where this is possible is the Little Caesar's Pizza in the Kmart. We usually visit the Kmart in Kaua'i at least twice on each of our stays. From souvenirs to reasonable groceries to the buying of forgotten sunscreen or flip flops etc., Kmart is a lifesaver. This brings us to the Little Caesars that is located inside Kmart and is a great place for a budget lunch or even dinner. A large pepperoni with bread sticks and wings will feed the whole family with some leftovers for not much over $20. A no-brainer! This trip can be combined with a trip to Costco, Ross, or even the Big Save Grocery store that share the same complex.

Fast Food and Gift Cards

There are many choices for fast food on Kaua'i, just like at home. One of our tricks to save money on vacation is to save up our gift cards throughout the year from birthdays and holidays for fast food restaurants. We enjoy them during our vacation to Kaua'i to keep the total budget for dining to a minimum.

CHAPTER 12: Dining In

Costco

4300 Nuhou St, Lihue

f you are shopping for groceries, Costco offers competitive prices, similar to what you might find on the mainland. We make this our first stop after landing in Kaua'i. It may not seem romantic to buy traditional groceries while on vacation, but neither is a large credit card bill from expensive restaurants! We plan on "eating out" only once per day, so having snacks, drinks, and easy-to-assemble meals on hand is a must to keep costs down.

Additionally, Costco sells discounted tickets to area attractions like "big ticket" boat ides to the Napali coast. If such luxurious adventurous are in your budget, buy the tickets t Costco at discounted prices in addition to reaping the 2% annual rebate on this purchase!

For a two-week vacation in Kaua'i, here is a breakdown of our families Costco shopping list:

Milk, eggs, bread, bacon, yogurt, premade salad, rotisserie chicken, celery, broccoli, Kirkland beer (yes, there is such a thing!), 3 flats of water, Chips, frozen chicken nuggets, Kirkland trail mix, Crustables, Diet Coke, Gatorade.

After you are done shopping at Costco, take a break and grab a picnic table. Truly the cheapest lunch on the island, the Costco hot dog and soda meal deal is the same price as you find on the mainland at just $1.50! You heard me, $1.50! The outdoor seating area also offers the usual Caesar salad, sandwiches, pizza, and smoothies at low prices.

Safeway: Deli counter and groceries

4454 Nahou St., Lihue

4-831 Kuhio Hwy, Kapaa

I consider myself a fried-chicken connoisseur, so when I proclaim that Safeway's deli counter offers the best bucket in the world, I want you to take me seriously. The new(er) Safeway at 4454 Nahou St., Lihue is "ah-mazing"! You can fill all of your stomachs with delicious hot food and fresh salads for a fraction of what you'd spend at area restaurants. Corn dog? Check. Fruit salad? Check. There is something for everyone! Safeway even offers a convenient seating area next to the deli and clean restrooms, all by the front door.

If you choose to load up on groceries during your visit (highly recommended!), be sure to swipe your Vons/Safeway club card for additional savings. If your hometown doesn't offer this grocery store chain, be sure to ask the cashier for an application. The rewards program is free and offers substantial in-store savings. Internet savvy shoppers can even "preload" digital coupons on their cards to take advantage of special sales. The prices at Safeway are extremely competitive to what you might see at home, and even offers programs you might be familiar with such as "Five Dollar Fridays." Lastly, look for the "manager's special" sticker attached to fresh seafood and meats for additional savings of 30-50% off the listed price. These "Manager Specials" are the marked-down meat, poultry and seafood that is close to expiration. There is a designated location in each of these sections in the store and I check these spots first when I shop Safeway at home or in Hawaii. I have NOT ONCE had an issue with these "close to expiration" meats, so I highly recommend looking here first. Of course, you must eat these the same day, or freeze them immediately when you get to your room.

Poke Bar

What's poke? Only my favorite food in the entire world. If you are not familiar with poke, let's start with the pronunciation. Poke rhymes with Okay, and is Hawaiian for "to section" or "to cut." Fishermen would cut-off slices from their catch and season them for snacks while working. Now the phenomenon of poke has traveled well beyond locals to the mainland where chain restaurants include poke on their menu.

While it may not look appetizing, this raw fish salad is served as an appetizer or even an entrée. Common ingredients are yellowfin tuna or ahi, raw salmon, octopus. Seasonings might include soy sauce, green onions, sesame oil, dried seaweed, chili pepper, fish eggs, or wasabi.

My personal favorite poke is served with chunks of avocado, a touch of wasabi, and is mixed with mayonnaise with a dash of soy sauce. A small container purchased at the grocery store deli (at upwards of $12/lb.) is pure heaven!

Big Save Markets (Times Supermarket)

Five locations:

9861 Waimea Rd., Waimea, HI

5516 Koloa Rd., Koloa, HI

5-5172 Kuhio Hwy, Hanalei

4-1105 Kuhio Hwy, Kapaa

4469 Waialo Rd., Eleele

Times Supermarket (Same corporation as Big Save Markets)

3-2600 Kaumualii Hwy, Lihue

Want to shop for your own groceries to save money, but still want to support Kaua'i businesses? Big Save Markets is one of Kaua'i's largest and oldest retailers having served Kaua'i for decades. This no-frills grocery store sells everything you would expect from a national chain, but on a smaller scale. We were surprised at many of the competitive prices – look for the yellow tag offering this week's specials. Highlights of Big Save are the poke bar (in the back near the seafood), hot deli (breakfast and lunch items), fresh bakery and plate lunch.

Barbecue locally caught fish

Koloa Fish Market

5482 Koloa Rd., Koloa

Monday-Friday 10-6, Saturday 10-5 (**cash only**)

Staying at a condo in Kaua'i? Most have a community barbecue pit where you can try your hand at preparing locally caught fresh fish. Not only will you save a wad of cash preparing a meal for your family, but the experience might just be the highlight of your vacation.

If you would rather take a pass on doing any cooking (you are on vacation after all,) rest assured that the Koloa Fish Market is happy to serve you a plate lunch or poke by the pound, ready for you to enjoy on the spot.

Whalers General Store

2360 Kiahuna Plantation Dr., Poipu

As we mentioned in the souvenir shopping section, Whalers General Store is a convenience store located in the Coconut Plantation Marketplace. It is a one-stop shop for snacks, coffee, cheap hot dogs, and maybe even a frozen pizza. If you don't feel like putting much effort into your meal, Whalers General Store can totally save you. The inexpensive coffee and morning pastries can hit the spot without breaking the bank. Check the open cooler areas to the right for fresh sandwiches, sushi, fresh fruit and other quick and easy meals on the go. You might even spot a manager's markdown if you look carefully!

CHAPTER 14:
Romance

L et me be clear that everything in Kaua'i is romantic! The lush tropical backdrop and relaxed lifestyle puts everyone in a good mood. That being said, here are a couple of "fancy pants" ideas to introduce some official "swankiness" to your vacation.

The Beach House: Order from the Lunch Menu

5022 Lawai Rd., Koloa

The Beach House located at 5022 Lawai Rd., Koloa boasts the most romantic view of any restaurant on the island! The open-aired tables face west, with unfettered views of the ocean, perfect for watching the sunset. This is the kind of restaurant where you "pop" the question or toast a wedding anniversary.

The dinner menu is outstanding but pricey! In order to afford this romantic destination, we make it a tradition of dressing up and enjoying an affordable lunch at the Beach House, eating the same delicious food -- at half the price — as the dinner menu. The waiters will even walk out onto the lush green lawn to take your group's picture. The views are priceless.

Honu Bar at Marriott's Waiohai Beach Club – Poipu

2249 Poipu Rd, Koloa

If you want to relax after a day in the sun golfing or just want a bite to eat while watching the sunset, this is THE place. As silly as it sounds, this place is my favorite hangout in all of Kaua'i. It's just magical. From the live music played seven days a week in the evenings, to the strolls on the nearby beach, and the moderately priced menu and cocktails, the Honu Bar is romance and relaxation epitomized!

Be sure to arrive an hour or so before sunset to get a table. Enjoy a dinner or just some cocktails or both. (The bar food menu is affordable and simple.) When the sun is about to set, you will notice the crowds moving north down the beachfront walkway toward a beautiful sunset. Take some selfies or get a passerby to snap a pic of your group.

It will probably come as a shock that once the sun sets (about 7:15 pm), the crowds will dissipate fairly quickly; the whole beach and grassy areas will become abandoned. This is just the nature of Kaua'i. This is the island that people choose for rest and relaxation, so once the sun goes down, everyone seems to rush back to their rooms to settle in. Maybe the Honu Bar, cocktails, live music and sunset are setting the stage for more romance?

CHAPTER 15:
Souvenir Shopping

Kmart

4303 Nawiliwili Rd in Lihue
7am-10pm

Kmart might be the best stop on the island for affordable new trinkets and souvenirs. They have several aisles devoted to Kauaʻi-stamped key chains, jewelry, t-shirts and more. The infamous "blue light specials" of Kmart often mark down popular items as "loss leaders" to draw you into the store, such as cutting the price of those chocolate-covered macadamia nuts that everyone likes to snack on!

Kmart carries aloha-styled merchandise throughout the store, so if your heart desires a bold hibiscus printed wrap or shirt, the prices here will likely beat the coastal souvenir shops by your hotel or resort.

The swimsuit selection at Kmart is spectacular and the sales are plentiful.

A few hints to enhance your shopping at Kmart include bringing the coupon from the advertisement Kmart runs in many activity brochures for a "free cloth bag with purchase." These large canvas bags come in handy when toting towels and such down to the pool, or even managing your overflow for the plane home. True cheapskates might even present the Kmart tote as an actual gift to their friends and family back home!

Additionally, be sure to sign up for the Kmart loyalty card program. With every purchase, the cash register prints an additional coupon for future use. We take advantage of the coupons by breaking up our purchases into smaller amounts, and applying the coupon to the next pile on the conveyer belt. You surely won't make friends with the folks in line behind you with this technique, so be forewarned!

Walmart

3-3300 Kuhio Hwy, Lihue

Everything is cheaper at Walmart! Says the shopper NOT stuck on an island. We were surprised to find that Walmart is NOT the loss leader of the island, and quite the contrary as they sometimes offered much higher prices than the same items at local grocery stores. Some of their food items came with a sticker shock like upwards of $8 for a favorite brand of cereal and north of $5 for a loaf of bread.

Their souvenir section was a tenth the size of Kmart, though their prices for tchotchkes remained competitive.

Walmart is still the most competitive for toiletries.

ABC Stores

The ABC Store has locations all over the island, and operates like a convenience store that also includes souvenirs. While the prices are higher than a larger grocery store, they will still be cheaper than your hotel restaurant or gift shop. Save your receipts from shopping at the ABC store as you earn a free gift after a certain dollar value is spent, like a free coffee cup after spending $50.

The ABC Store sells everything from cigars and hard alcohol to toothpaste and Gatorade. More often than not you can walk to one of these stores from your hotel or condo and be in and out in just a few minutes.

Whalers General Store

2360 Kiahuna Plantation Dr., Suite E10-50, Koloa

4-4350 Kuhio Hwy, Anahola

Would you rather spend $25 or $5 for the same necklace? Many of the same trinkets can be found at various stores around the island, but at very different prices! Whaler's is located next to Starbucks, Keoki's Paradise and other island favorites in the Poipu shopping center at 2360 Kiahuna Plantation Dr., Suite E10-50, Koloa

Like a small convenience store (but much nicer!), Whaler's sells alcohol (beer, wine, hard alcohol), snacks, souvenirs, and gifts – everything a tourist needs if you are too lazy from beach combing to make it into town. There is a small fresh food refrigerator section that offers homemade sandwiches, snacks, and even sushi depending on when you stop by. We have even seen the manager slap 50% off stickers onto food items in this section as the clock ticks by!

My daughter (the expert souvenir shopper) claims Whaler's is competitive and unique in their merchandise. She specifically calls out the jewelry, Hawaiian books, keychains and t-shirts as the crème de la crème of Kaua'i. I am always on the lookout for something unique to bring home, and on my last trip to Whaler's I purchased a hand-quilted pillow cover by local artists for a crisp $20 bill.

Instead of paying $10 for dessert at one of the restaurants in this shopping center, consider stopping by Whaler's for an ice cream or popsicle treat. Combine that with a Red-Box movie rental, and you have yourself a couple of hours of recuperation.

Maui Divers Jewelry Store

3416 Rice St #201, Lihue

Located south of the Marriott in Lihue at the shopping center which houses the ABC Store, the Maui Divers Jewelry Store offers a fun free gimmick to lure in customers. Every guest gets to try a key to open a treasure chest to win a prize. Visit whenever you are in the area as you can play once a day.

CHAPTER 16:
Souvenir Shopping &
Thrift Stores

Before you pay full price for a Kaua'i t-shirt or hat, be sure to check out the selection at the area thrift stores. I suspect area hotels donate their lost-and-found here, as there is always a plethora of sun hats, swim suits, t-shirts, and flip flops for sale, many of which are imprinted with Kaua'i logos and designs.

Habitat for Humanity

1-3410 Kaumualii Hwy, Hanapepe

Not known for ample parking or even a public bathroom, the Habitat for Humanity Thrift Store is a treasure hunt of fun. The store sells completely random donated household items, so you can't go in with specific expectations.

We love being able to say YES YOU CAN HAVE THAT to our kids as they load inexpensive games, DVDs, puzzles and books into our cart for pennies on the dollar. It rains a lot in Kaua'i, and having activities the kids can do in the room is priceless.

Additionally, we've come across bikes, scooters, surf boards, boogie boards that would be cheaper to buy here than rent from your hotel. When your vacation is over you can just leave at your hotel lobby or inside your condo to pay it forward.

Now we realize that thrift store shopping isn't for everyone. This might be taking your cheapskate nature to a whole new level of thriftiness. Before you pass judgement, I beg you to stop by and take a peak!

Kaua'i Humane Society: Blooming Tales Resale Store

3178 Kuhio Hwy, Lihue

The Kaua'i Humane Society Thrift Shop sells goods ranging from clothing to toys to electronics, all benefiting the Humane Society. This is a very clean, bright, and well-organized store with a nice staff. To describe it in short would be a small boutique style thrift store. No bathrooms are available, so plan ahead!

CHAPTER 17:
Community Events

Garden Island Artisan Fair

Happens - Quarterly on the 6th Saturday 9am – 3 pm

Poipu Beach Park, 2179 Hoone Rd., Koloa

f you are lucky enough to be visiting Kaua'i when the quarterly craft fair is being held (currently around the 6th Saturday of the quarter), be sure to plan your excursions with this event at the forefront. Held in the dirt parking lot area near Brennecke's and Poipu beach, the craft fair is a "flea market" style free event where you can interact with artisans, locals, and craftsmen. While some of the merchandise is the typical "made in China" trinkets that are the same in every souvenir shop, most of the offerings are one-of-a kind, handmade treasures with a modest price tag to match! If you are like me, sometimes you come across that special item that you know you will treasure for decades to come, and this is the place to find such items.

Hanapepe Art Walk

Hanapepe, South Shore – West of Koloa

Have you seen the Disney movie "Lilo and Stitch"? You might remember the characters Lilo and Nani are from the sleepy rural town of Hanapepe, located on the southern side of Kaua'i. In fact, a tribute mural outside the vintage Aloha Theatre beckons Disney fans to take a selfie.

Every Friday night from 5-9pm, Hanapepe artists and businesses welcome the community to a free gathering. Art galleries are open late, music fills the air, and even food trucks tempt you to try local cuisine. Parking is a free for all on the side of Hanapepe Road just off Kaumualii Hwy.

Hanapepe calls itself "Kaua'i's biggest little town," and they aren't exaggerating. It's a one street show from the Wild West with lots of dust sprinkled with a little charm. Among the handful of artisan shops, our favorite is the Aloha Spice Factory. They offer a very clean public bathroom (so important people!) and unique affordable souvenirs. I am still enjoying the jar of coconut macadamia peanut butter I bought last summer! You can recreate the flavors of the island by bringing home Hawaiian spices – the gift that keeps on giving.

I'm a sucker for hand-made art as opposed to the "made in China" knickknacks sold in most of the Kaua'i gift shops. The Banana Patch Studio in Hanapepe offer unique hand painted ceramic tiles, pottery and fine art at prices us common folks on a budget can afford. You can even watch the many artists at work through the glass divider in the adjacent studio space. This is just one of the 16 galleries that will entice and entertain you.

Before leaving Hanapepe, be sure to explore the swinging bridge. This historic wooden bridge will raise your blood pressure ever-so-slightly as it swoons and creaks as your weight shifts. Crossing the Hanapepe River, Kaua'i's third largest river, the bridge basically takes you nowhere. There is nothing on the other side worth exploring! Still, the bridge is free, fun, and part of local history, not to mention will make you feel like a kid again.

We wouldn't be cheapskates if we admitted actually eating dinner at the Hanapepe Friday Night Art Walk. Just a few miles away is the McDonald's 4469 Waialo Rd. in Eleele, where you can even enjoy the tastes of the islands by ordering Taro Pie for dessert.

Kauaʻi Community Market

3-1901 Kaumualii Hwy, Lihue

Saturdays, 930-100pm on the front lawn and parking lot at the Kauaʻi Community College

Koloa Plantation Days

Every July, Koloa celebrates its 100-year-old heritage of the immigrants whose sweat and tears fueled the sugar industry. The family friendly celebration includes a variety of activities, most of which can be enjoyed for free and outdoors. Traditions, music, dances and food will be honored from immigrant backgrounds of the Philippines, Europe, the Azores, Japan, Korea, China and more. Current schedule of upcoming events and how you might like to participate can be found on their website: www.koloaplantationdays.com

Bon Dance – Festival

Typically held from June through August, the Obon or Bon festival is a traditional Buddhist ceremony to honor the spirit of one's ancestors. This spectacular cultural display is not unique to Kauaʻi, but a fascinating celebration of the Japanese going back over 500 years.

Please check with the Kauaʻi Japanese Society for exact times and locations.

Concerts

https://kauaifestivals.com/

Depending on the time of your visit, there are often free music or cultural festivals available. Because they change and are updated regularly, we are unable to specify each event. However, we suggest looking into concerts at the following locations:

Slack Key Guitar & Ukulele Concerts

Hanalei Community Center, Hanalei

Hanalei All Saints' Church, Kapaa

Or even better, learn to play the ukulele while on vacation. There is a terrific ukulele store across from Walmart called Scotty's Music House where you can ask questions and road test different models. I drove my family crazy practicing IZ for hours!

Free Movie Night

Anaina Hou Community Park, Kilauea and various locations – look for signs

CHAPTER 18: Final Words

Vacation planning can be stressful and expensive. We hope that by sharing our many years of experience on the island can help to relieve some of the pressure for your trip planning. We wanted to highlight some, but not all, of the free and cheap ways to enjoy your vacation. You only have a limited amount of time on your vacation, so we did highlight free/cheap places that unworthy of your time. Of course, there are always new places or businesses to explore, and ideas to share with one another, so if you come across something you feel should be included in the next edition of Kauaʻi Cheap Vacations, please reach out to us!

When all is said and done, your memories from Kauaʻi will be of the time you spent together, not the money you spent. Until next time…If you enjoyed this book, please help others find it by leaving an honest review on Amazon. Remember, proceeds benefit the Kauai Humane Society, so you are also helping furry friends back on the island!

Mahalo and Aloha!

Bill, Stephanie, Charlotte and Alexander Laska

30200545R00104

Made in the USA
San Bernardino, CA
22 March 2019